EBIZ SCAMS REVEALED

Ultimate Guide to Avoiding Scams

For
Work at Home
eBiz Owners

CHRIS MALTA

DEDICATION

To my students, who understand that real education
has always been the key to personal success.

CONTENTS

ACKNOWLEDGMENTS

Thanks to Marian, who also believes people need to know these things; without her constant cheerleading and editorial efforts this book would not exist..

INTRODUCTION

I'm Chris Malta.

If you're among an estimated 65 percent of Americans who dream of earning money online—as a side-gig, or for extra retirement income, or to replace current full-time income, selling products, services or something else—you're painting a giant target on your back for "Ropers" in a huge network of con artists.

I'm here to help you avoid that.

Why should you take my advice when it comes to learning how to avoid complex scams ranging from "How to sell on Amazon.com" to "private labeling" to "sourcing from China" to "retail arbitrage" and many more fraudulent schemes involving home-based, e-commerce business opportunities? Or pay attention to what I tell you about how things truly work in the world of real e-commerce business startups? Or listen to me as I teach how to actually build a profitable online business?

Lots of reasons.

I've spent more than 25 years building successful businesses in all aspects of e-commerce. I've been teaching e-commerce in various ways since the early 2000's and have offered students more than 7,000 hours of live mentoring. I also offer free education through my detailed, 11-part <u>EBiz Insider Video Series</u> (see end notes to find it[1] and rated 4.9/5 by Trustpilot[2]).

I've watched the "home based businesses on the internet" industry evolve in many different ways.

I've seen some good things over time, but also a tremendous amount of bad, in the people and processes involved in this field. I've studied both and have publicly spoken about both.

I'm writing this book not only for people who are driven to earn money online. Unfortunately, many of them may plunge into the "potential scam victim pool." People who may know and love someone who's begun spending money (or is considering doing so) on "business opportunities," may have faced or facing situations that may be too good to be true. If that sounds like someone you care about, it might be time to ask some hard questions.

Looking at one new estimate of at least 30 million people in the U.S. alone, who are actively involved in or planning to start a business[3], it's likely that you or someone you know, may be among them.

That estimate doesn't include—as I mentioned earlier—the millions more who are just thinking about the idea of starting a business to make money online.

After all, for many people, owning a business is one version of "The American Dream." Experience has shown me that the pool of potential scam victims is far deeper than most people realize.

In the course of talking to and teaching this business to thousands of people over the years, I've heard many horror stories about the financial and emotional havoc these e-commerce con artists wreak upon their victims.

Stories about these predators, their tactics and their victims need to be told, for the sake of people who might someday become prey, those who don't yet know they're being devoured and those who have already met their fates in the bellies of the beasts.

Many of my students—who are interviewed throughout this book—have stated that before we met, they were indeed swindled by some of these evil clowns. Most of those students lost tens of thousands of dollars.

I was able to give some of them information about how to get refunds. For others, it was just too late.

I sincerely hope it isn't too late for you and those you care about; that this book will help you spot those con artists and—while I'll never tell you it's an easy road—if you decide that you'd like more information about building a real online business—I'll be here to help you do it right.

1 THE HUNT

As I said in my Introduction, the minute you start searching the internet for information about how to start a business from home, you've painted a gigantic target on your back that says, "Here I am. Please lie to me and cheat me out of all my money."

You need to know this, because according to some reports, consumer fraud in the United States has gone up by more than 60 percent since 2008.   Online scams have more than doubled.[4]

Added to that, the FBI—according to its Internet Crime Complaint Center—claims that Internet-enabled theft, fraud, and exploitation—including pyramid schemes disguised as home-based business opportunities—are still widespread and were responsible for a staggering $2.7 billion in financial losses in 2018, alone.[5]

You need to know how to avoid being hit, and what may help if it's already happened to you. That's what this book is about.

That said, I'm not going to just give you a "short list of tips" to avoid being scammed, or offer up "7 Ways to Deal With" the aftermath of a business opportunity scam.

Instead, I'll dissect the when, where and how of the Scammers' cunning and corrupt schemes. Why? Because—aside from staying out of the water—one of the best ways to avoid a shark-attack is to understand how sharks hunt and act accordingly.

While writing this book, I interviewed many people throughout the United States who, like over 30 million others in the U.S., are actively pursuing the "American Dream" of small business ownership.[6]

All of them are intelligent, educated consumers.

A gigantic hidden network of sophisticated con artists who sold them what seemed like legitimate, home-based, business opportunities outrageously scammed all of them.

At the time they were scammed, each interviewee was interested in starting an online e-commerce business. (The term "e-commerce" refers to buying or selling products or services over the internet.) In some of their cases, that meant learning to sell products on Amazon.com or eBay, importing from China, "private labeling", "retail arbitrage" and many more supposedly "easy" ways to make money from home.

Excerpts from those interviews are scattered throughout these chapters to help you avoid the very subtle, polished scamming that— in the hands of horrifically unscrupulous experts—easily defeats your innate sense of caution and common sense and can cause irreversible financial damage to your life, as well as the lives of many people among an estimated *65 percent*[7] of Americans who dream of earning a full-time or supplementary income as a small business owner.

These evil clowns don't care who they hurt, either. They have no second thoughts about going after cash-strapped millennials, retirees, people planning for retirement, members of the military and its veterans, the unemployed, the disabled, people who do not speak English as their first language and more.

Joanell, for example, is still trying to recover from near economic ruin. She's a student of mine who lives in Connecticut. Before I met her, she was an assistant vice president in a financial division of a large corporation. Her division was shut down by that corporation and she was desperate to replace at least part of her income in a tough job market. She turned to the promises of an e-commerce business information marketer and lost over $30,000 at a time when she was most vulnerable.

When I interviewed her, Joanell said, "It was me Googling, searching and I found somebody who was selling a ready-made Website. All products (to sell) were there, I gave 'em so much money and then I never heard from them again. I couldn't find them; I couldn't Google them. They just disappeared. Completely. Eventually I lost my home. I had a condominium, but I couldn't find work other than a dog daycare temporarily and lost the condo. Now I rent a room in someone's house."

Mark, another student of mine, is from Houston, Texas. He's been a cabinetmaker, a landscaper and a musician in a local band. He went back to school, earned a degree and became a public-school teacher, instructing his own students for the next 22 years. Nearing retirement age, he dreamed of owning a profitable business so that he could better provide for his family after he retired. He investigated how to earn money-selling products online through e-commerce and before I met him, he was cheated out of $37,000 in less than a year, with no business to show for it.

According to Mark, "The guy that led the workshop, his name was Randolph. Lily, who was my 'financial advisor', got me signed up with credit cards to be able to pay $22,000. I have never heard from either one of these people since. In fact, I actually called this guy Randolph. Because he said, 'Here's my personal number, you call can me anytime.' And I said, 'I've got a couple questions for you.' He said he had to run to get on a plane, 'let me get back to you.' That's been a year ago. I still haven't heard from him."

These are just two examples of people whose hopes and dreams were dashed, and their lives shattered, because they trusted people who said they would help them build a better future for themselves by starting an online business.

The minute they used the internet to begin exploring the launch of a home-based business—and I mean the very minute they began to investigate—"The Hunt" began as well.

They were the prey and if you're interested starting a business to sell a product or service on Amazon.com, eBay or any other online outlet—so are you.

You'll have lots of company.

According to a 2019 U.S. survey, nearly *two-thirds*[8] of Americans dream of opening a small business, while a smaller, but still substantial percentage of Americans are actually in the process of launching a business or have already opened their doors.

The Global Entrepreneurship Monitor, an academic organization that investigates entrepreneurship around the world, estimates that in 2018, nearly *16 percent* of working-age Americans (Ages 18-64) was actively involved in business startups.

Those people were either planning the launch of their businesses, or hard at work during their business's first three-and-a-half years.

That statistic means that in 2018, *about 31 million American adults—nearly 10 percent of the entire U.S. population*—were actively pursuing the American dream of becoming an entrepreneur.

Unfortunately, for those who are nurturing the idea of starting a company, business opportunity fraud—including work-at-home schemes—is one of the *Top 10 fraud categories* reported by the Federal Trade Commission's Consumer Sentinel Network (CSN).

The Federal Trade Commission's "CSN" is a huge law enforcement database containing millions of complaints compiled by consumer advocacy agencies and entities across the United States; agencies like state attorneys general, the Better Business Bureau and scam watchers like AARP.[9]

In addition to ranking business opportunity fraud as high on its fraud list, CSN also shows that average individual losses—because of that type of fraud— were the *second highest* of all reported fraud.

Who are the victims? Scammed entrepreneurs can be any age and want to start a business for many reasons, but FTC court cases—many of which are mentioned in this book—as well as surveys and reports show that several specific groups may be more susceptible to the widespread scamming that these e-commerce con artists are involved in.

As briefly mentioned earlier, many so-called millennials—people born between 1981 and 1996—who are struggling under crushing student loan debt, are desperately searching for supplemental income in the "gig economy." Unfortunately searching online for ways to make that happen is like sending out a mass invitation *to be ripped off.*

There is nothing good about that, but at least, according to the

FTC, members of that age group are 25 percent *more likely to report* being scammed than is anyone over the age of 40.[10]

That increases the possibility that the con artist who scammed a millennial may actually be *caught.*

However, that also means that at least *25 percent* of e-commerce frauds inflicted against people over the age of 40 *don't get reported.*

That's not good news for anyone who's trying to catch the Scammers, especially because there are plenty of victims in that "over 40" age group.

According to the Second Annual "Inside Small Business Survey" commissioned by The UPS Store, *fully half* of Americans would prefer opening a small business rather than just retiring.[11]

That independent survey also reveals "both optimism and fear" associated with opening a small business.

Having been born and raised in a family of businesspeople, I can tell you that there's plenty to be nervous about for those would-be entrepreneurs; like having money for basic operating costs, supplies and equipment. But what *didn't* make the list of "feared expenses," was the possibility of a surprise attack by the bottom-feeders of the e-commerce "Scam World." It *should* have.

Most of us would think that people who are trained to *fend off* attacks would be well equipped to avoid them, but that isn't the case with the next group of likely e-commerce scam victims; members of the U.S. military. They too, are targets of business opportunity fraud, which is also among the Top 10 frauds inflicted upon members of the Armed Services. In fact, the number of frauds reported by military men and women is *higher* than the number reported by the general public.[12]

Veterans of the military are another group who are heavily targeted by the e-commerce Scammers because they can be more susceptible to the frauds. The same is true of people who've lost their jobs, and people who do not speak English as their first language.

Disabled people, including men and women injured in U.S. military combat, are also targets and—as you'll see—their injuries can be particularly cruel, especially if they are scammed as a result of disgraceful marketing practices that include ads mentioning "brained damaged people." You'll soon see an example of just that.

The Scammers' "no limits" behavior also expands beyond geographical boundaries. U.S. con artists will sometimes team up with citizens of foreign countries who will never play by U.S. law enforcement rules.

The History of Work-at-Home Con Artistry

Home-based (work-from-home) business opportunities have been the center of a vast epidemic of scams for a long time.

Just one example, from the early 20th century, is the envelope-stuffing frauds that started in the 1920's and promised $2 for each envelope stuffed with written material. In that Scammers' sinister "stroke of genius," the home-based worker was charged $2 to get *into* the scam, and was then told to stuff envelopes with a flier for *the scam itself*—and try and get $2 from *other* local people for it.

Some of the many other work-from-home schemes over the years have included the following categories.

Craft and other product assembly at home is small business to pay up front for the product, assemble it and sell it back to the company, at which time people were told the product didn't meet assembly standards.

Medical billing-from-home is another (paying for the courses and then find out that no medical companies would hire a home-based biller).

Gold-Brick Scams is still another one (sales of products for more than they're worth).

Multiple pyramid scams and multilevel marketing schemes have always been one (business models that recruit members through promises of payments for enrolling others into the scheme)[13]

Phone sex scams, many more types, and other categories.

Historically, these frauds have been advertised in newspapers and magazines, but with the explosion of the internet, the Scammers' former advertising on paper media—as well as the tired old scams they promoted—has "virtually" disappeared.

Where the Scammers' Shadow Industry is Now

Advertising on the world wide web is now the promotion of choice for con artists whose carefully disguised schemes are primarily focused on e-commerce and the idea of making money online from home.

There is a massive global shadow industry of scam operators who, in the United States alone, generate well over a billion dollars a year (and likely far more; no one tracks the exact number) by *knowingly* cheating people out of their money in the ecommerce information market.

They're not the subject of national media stories and if negative information about them is posted online, they'll spend millions of dollars suppressing it.

I want to be clear about why I call these operations scams. A few of my reasons are as follows:

They usually break one or more federal and state laws in the way they recruit consumers (promising unsubstantiated "six-figure incomes" in a short period, violating business opportunity rules, illegal telemarketing, etc.)

Some teach business methods that are simply ridiculous in the real world.

Others teach methods that make absolutely no sense for home-based business owners in particular.

All of them are purposely set up to give consumers very little useful information.

They promise to provide *more* information over a long period of time, while they trick consumers into spending more and more money until they have nothing left to spend.

Many of the people who run them know all this and they do it on purpose.

The overworked and underfunded Federal Trade Commission (FTC) isn't equipped to track down and take legal action against every one of these cheats, particularly because, as mentioned, these U.S. citizens sometimes have counterparts overseas who are nearly impossible to prosecute. That's one reason it's difficult to shut down these operations before the damage has been done.

If you start exploring this business, you are guaranteed to run into these villains, but it's likely that you won't recognize their cons until it's too late.

The chance of encountering risky information vendors goes up because they are looking for you, regardless of whether you want to investigate product sales through eBay, Amazon, or your own website. They'll also hunt you down if you make your own products and want to learn how to sell them, or if you want to investigate how to earn cash blogging, or profitably creating videos for YouTube, or through affiliate marketing, information sales, and a dozen other "money making opportunities."

No matter what you think you want to do, the minute you start asking questions, thousands upon thousands of hungry predators will instantly smell blood in the water, and the pursuit will begin. It will not end well for their prey.

One particularly sad example of that is the story of Mike, his wife Sandy and their recently deceased son.

During my interview with the couple, Sandy said, "We had a disabled son, and we wanted to do something where he could work with us, and I wanted my husband to be working at home with me. Our overall cost, including inventory that is now in our house…it's about $15,000. We had to try to make (it) work until we just had to *stop*."

They will find you. Once you hand over your contact information, you won't be able to hide. Your email address, phone number and personal information will be illegally traded and sold repeatedly, within a massive system of hidden relationships between these merciless trackers. Your email inbox will explode with "amazing offers" claiming that you can make your dreams come true with hundreds of different "money making systems". Your phone will start to ring, and extremely skilled, high-pressure telemarketers will start hammering you with offer after seductive offer.

It will never end.

These "Hunters" are not just individuals. They're big companies, too; very well respected internet concerns that you'd never suspect of being so very bad for you.

They all operate on a single underlying premise. They all strongly believe that most people are too stupid to build, own and run a real business of any kind. They view would-be entrepreneurs—who are trying to achieve the American Dream of business ownership--as simple grunts. Worker bees. Hourly wage slaves with no idea what they're doing when it comes to business; ignoramuses who will believe *anything* they're told.

It's like a virtual cattle drive. If you wander into their territory, they'll do anything they need to do and say anything they need to say, to herd you and thousands of other consumers into the slaughterhouse pens every week.

The blood they plan to drain in that slaughterhouse is *all of your money*.

Take a moment and think about everything you own. Your bank accounts. Your savings. Retirement plans. Your kids' college funds. Your home. Right down to the quarters, nickels and dimes in your change jar.

Then imagine all of it...*gone*. Everything. Forever. With nowhere left to go and absolutely nothing to show for it.

This is the carefully planned and mercilessly executed plan they have for you. Yes, you *personally*, because even after they get to know you, they don't see you as a fellow human being

Again, they know what they're doing to you, they have meetings, discuss tactics to victimize you, and they simply *do not care the slightest bit* about what happens to you after every cent you have is gone and you're still in exactly the same place you were when "The Hunt" started; no home-based business whatsoever.

Except that now, besides losing the opportunity to start a real home-based business, you're also *broke*.

When they finally drain you to the point when there's nothing left to drain, they'll leave you with a little parting gift as well; a mountain of credit card debt that *they encouraged* and that you can't *pay*.

Do you think I'm exaggerating? Does it sound like conspiracy theory? Something that couldn't possibly happen to *you*? That you have a good sense of what's real or fake and nobody could ever fool you to such an extent?

If that's what you think, just look at the following ads, which reportedly helped rake in at least $300 million[14] for alleged bottom-feeding con artists who—according to the FTC—sold bogus online business opportunities with laser- focused advertising aimed at members of the U.S. Armed Services, veterans and retirees.

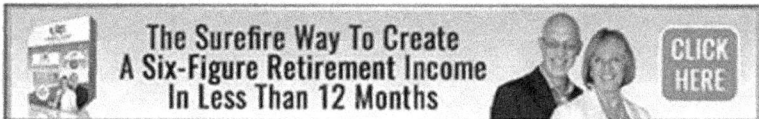

Source of Images: FTC v. Mobe Ltd., et al –
UNITED STATES DISTRICT COURT MIDDLE DISTRICT OF FLORIDA

Like I said, e-commerce business opportunity fraudsters will do and say anything necessary to make a wicked deal—including the use of marketing tactics that exploit people with disabilities, patriotic soldiers and seniors living on fixed incomes.

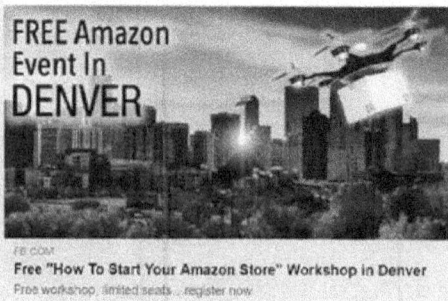

FREE Amazon Event In DENVER

FB.COM
Free "How To Start Your Amazon Store" Workshop in Denver
Free workshop, limited seats... register now

In many instances, they act like 21st Century versions of traveling "snake oil" peddlers, setting up their wares in cities across the United States and Canada, after having advertised their free "business opportunity shows" using email and social media outlets like

Facebook and Instagram.

According to a United States District Court claim filed by the Federal Government and the Minnesota Attorney General, two such companies and their representatives advertised and held two-hour live "seminars" or "workshops" in 66 U.S. and Canadian cities.[15]

The agencies stated that all of the events were intended to "lure consumers" into purchasing a bogus system intended to teach them *"How To Start Your Own Online Amazon Store...Even Starting With No Product, No Inventory, No Tech Know-How And Without Having To Ship Anything Yourself..."*

According to the FTC, these "traveling salesmen" and their companies "deceptively offered consumers a 'full-service, turnkey package'" while making earnings claims that were false and unsubstantiated.

CASE 0:18-cv-02207-DWF-TNL Document 1 Filed 07/30/18 Page 1 of 54

UNITED STATES DISTRICT COURT
DISTRICT OF MINNESOTA

FEDERAL TRADE COMMISSION, and	
STATE OF MINNESOTA, by its Attorney General, Lori Swanson,	CASE NO. 18 Sc 2207 DWF/TNL

> 79. Defendants have conducted Sellers Playbook live events throughout the United States including in Albuquerque, Anaheim, Anchorage, Atlanta, Atlantic City, Austin, Baltimore, Boise, Boston, Buffalo, Charleston, Charlotte, Chicago, Cincinnati, Cleveland, Columbus, Dallas, Denver, Des Moines, Detroit, El Paso, Fort Lauderdale, Fort Myers, Fort Wayne, Fort Worth, Grand Rapids, Hartford, Honolulu, Houston, Indianapolis, Jacksonville, Kansas City, Las Vegas, Lincoln, Long Beach, Long Island, Los Angeles, Louisville, Memphis, Miami, Milwaukee, Nashville, New York City, Newark, Norfolk, Oklahoma City, Orlando, Palm Springs, Philadelphia, Phoenix, Pittsburgh, Raleigh, Reno, Richmond, Sacramento, Salt Lake City, San Antonio, San Diego, San Francisco, San Jose, Seattle, Saint Louis, Tampa, Tucson, Washington DC, and Wichita.

Persuading the Skeptics

A good con artist is an expert at convincing skeptics that a "seems-to-good-to-be-true" offer really does represent a legitimate way to start a business.

In 1945, the French philosopher Alexandre Koyre wrote, "The mob believes everything it is told, provided only that it be repeated over and over." This is simply psychology, and it's absolutely correct. But it goes back much further than 1945.

The art of the scam, the trade of "The Hunters," goes back to the dawn of human history. There have always been predators and there will always be prey, in both the physical and the psychological sense.

Now, in this fast-paced digital world, the art of the scam has been perfected and repeated so often that it's nearly impossible to escape. "The Hunters" dominate, and their prey suffers for it.

But you do have a chance to survive "The Hunt," because *The Hunters" have always had one thing wrong.* Contrary to what they believe, most people who are interested in entrepreneurship are *not* stupid.

If you're among the 65 percent who dream of starting their own companies and you want to earn an *internet-based* income, you can learn to build a real business. First, though, you have to learn to evade *"The Hunters,"* and that's not easy.

In this book, I'm going to expose the basic anatomy of the Scammers' cons, the mind games, the warning signs and the words and methods used by "The Hunters."

You'll also be reading more excerpts from my interviews with people who have been horrendously scammed. They will tell you their sometimes-heartbreaking stories themselves.

Why? They said that if telling their stories would help others avoid a similar fate, they were willing to revisit and talk about their painful past.

As my student Mark put it, "I'm willing to do whatever I can to help... I'd love to see some kind of justice come from all this, because I do believe this guy was a scam artist."

If you make a *conscious decision to educate yourself,* pay close attention to the Scammers' techniques and remember these real-life examples, you can survive "The Hunt" and—armed with the truth about e-commerce—you can actually prosper.

So, you have a choice. You can learn, right now, how this hidden, shameless scam, fraud and swindles machine works—so that you can completely avoid it—or you can amble into the pen with the herd and learn to say

"M-o-o-o-o..."

2 THE GRIFTERS

According to Merriam-Webster,[16] the word "grift" is defined as follows:

Grift
verb
\ ˈgrift \
grifted; grifting; grifts
Definition of grift
transitive verb
: to obtain (money or property) illicitly (as in a confidence game)
intransitive verb
: to acquire money or property illicitly

The word "Grifter" first found its way into our modern vocabulary in 1915, in George Bronson-Howard's novel, *God's Man*, in which Bronson-Howard writes: "Grifting ain't what it used to be. Fourteenth Street's got protection down to a system – a regular underworld tariff on larceny."

A "Grifter" was described as a "confidence man" ... any criminal who relied on skill and wits instead of violence.

In this book, and in my articles, blog posts, videos and podcasts on this subject, I call them "Scammers," but the definition remains the same.

Note the word *criminal* in the above reference.

In the online world of home-based e-commerce information marketing, there are three kinds of Scammers:

1. Those who are actual law-breaking criminals.
2. Those who are moral lawbreakers and
3. Those who are too ignorant to know they're scamming.

All three will hunt you down with equally gleeful enthusiasm, and all three will hurt you equally badly. There are thousands upon thousands of them in the search engines and throughout the social media platforms.

They will promise you everything you desire from a home-based ecommerce business, and I imagine then they'll figuratively crap all over your head and laugh while you thank them for the hat.

Nearly every last one of them knows beyond any doubt that the fish-bait dangling in front of your nose will not work for you. But that doesn't matter to them, because you're just a fish, and who cares?

Let's take a closer look at these three types of morally under-developed life forms:

The Lawbreaking Scammers

From the small fly-by-night Scammers who take your money and run, to the big convention-hall rah-rah session operators who advertise in social media, newspapers and on local TV, the lawbreakers are getting harder to pin down, despite their visibility to those who want to start an online business.

Why? Because of their lawyers.

Yep, they're lawyering up, and those lawyers are writing—in print so small that you need an electron microscope to see it—all kinds of legal "get out of jail free" stipulations into their contracts.

Very few people actually read the fine print when they sign with these "jack wagons"—to throw away their kids' college funds or their retirement money—and even fewer people own an electron microscope.

They *say* one thing; you *sign* another. Then, they leave you in a ditch while they're beating their *next* victim over the head.

There are, however, Scammers who are as stupid as they are morally bankrupt, and they *do* get caught. Not too long ago, the FTC put a stop to an operation run by two brothers from Massachusetts who were charging people up to $35,000 to tell them they could make tons of money as a home-based business owner selling on Amazon.

The Federal Trade commission didn't just shut down their operation. The FTC also took them to U.S. District Court for breaking two laws; the Federal Trade Commission Act and the Business Opportunity Rule. They were also sued by Amazon *itself* and by the Washington State Attorney General, who filed a consumer protection lawsuit.

From *Cnet*[17] (June 8, 2018): (Excerpt)

FTC reaches $11M settlement with get-rich-quick scammers targeting Amazon

Authorities said Adam and Christopher Bowser duped some prospective Amazon sellers for thousands of dollars each.

The Federal Trade Commission on Monday[18] it reached a $10.8 million settlement with two brothers who allegedly scammed prospective Amazon sellers for years with bogus coaching advice.

Adam and Christopher Bowser, who live in Massachusetts, agreed to the settlement[19] after the FTC charged the brothers in March.[20] The federal watchdog alleged the two were running the scam using their business, FBA Stores. Jody Marshall, who is listed as a coach for the Bowsers' business, was also part of the settlement. The agency will work to give back payments to those harmed by the scam.

As part of the settlement, the defendants neither admitted nor denied the allegations against them and got the bulk of a $102 million judgment against them suspended. They were also barred from future business coaching...

Amazon and Washington State's attorney general filed separate suits against the Bowsers in December and were working with the FTC on its case.

Amazon is aggressively fighting bad and illegal practices on its websites and services. The company has already pursued fake reviewers,[21] sellers of counterfeit products[22] and alleged fraudsters on its Kindle Direct Publishing platform.[23] Going after FBA Stores could help Amazon show it's working to protect small businesses from such practices, too.

"We will continue to aggressively pursue those who harm our customer and seller experience," the company said in a statement Monday.

According to the Washington state filing, the Bowser brothers **were running an alleged scam since 2009**. They drew in people by **offering free webinars or in-person workshops on how to sell on Amazon** and routinely used Amazon's logos in their signs and brochures, the suit said, though they had no affiliation with Amazon. At these events, they persuaded people to pay $1,000 for three-day workshops.

At the workshops, they allegedly used **aggressive sales tactics to get people to register for more coaching or seminars,** which cost from $4,000 for the "Wholesale" package, **up to $35,000 for the "Diamond Coaching Package."**

However, many of the tips the Bowsers offered violate Amazon's terms of service and could result in sellers getting banned, the state suit alleged. The FTC also claimed most, **if not all**, purchasers didn't earn the income the Bowsers advertised, which was to make $5,000 to $10,000 a month

The **bold emphasis** in the above article from *CNet* is mine.

While the *CNet* article explains some of what these people do to get themselves caught and prosecuted, there's a lot more on that list.

Here is an example of an advertised workshop endorsement that appeared in the State of Washington's consumer protection lawsuit against the Bowser brothers and their companies:

> My name is Adam Bowser, and over the past 18 years I have sold over $50 million online. I'm going to be hosting a few local workshops around the Seattle area to share my secrets for making money on Amazon . . . I personally sold over $12 million on Amazon last year and this exclusive program is limited to the first 100 registrants.

In the State of Washington's claim, the attorney general alleged, "Defendants engage in unfair and deceptive acts or practices...by giving consumers the net impression that Defendants have developed strategies, secrets, insider knowledge, or expertise that will result in substantial financial gain for purchasers of their business opportunities."

That language of the lawsuit is civilized compared to what the State of Washington's attorney general said was contained in the duo's alleged email advertising; "The emails promise consumers that they will "discover the secrets to making a 'stinking fortune' on Amazon."

But would they? The attorney general disagreed, stating, "Most Washington consumers who purchase Defendants' business opportunities will not develop a successful online business as promised, earn little or no income, and may end up heavily in debt as a result."

AWS
Amazing Wealth Systems

My Goal is To Show You How You Can Make an Additional $5,000-$10,000 Per Month Spending about 5-10hrs A Week

Figure 2 – FBA Webinar

Who were those consumers? The lawsuit identified many workshop attendees as people who were "retired, students, or do not speak English as their first language."

Meanwhile, over in Nevada U.S.

District Court, the FTC was giving everyone a hint about the huge amount of money that goes into marketing and orchestrating events like the FBA workshops, which focused on selling what the founders named, "Amazing Wealth Systems."

Take a look at what the FTC claimed was an ad for an exclusive "summit" in—where else? Las Vegas!

Live Amazon 4-Day Summit

To Register Call **909-340-9974** immediately!

Seating is limited to the first 500 registrants.

Attend Our Summit and

Learn How to Make Amazing Wealth Using Amazon

FOUR DAYS!

LAS VEGAS

NOVEMBER 3-6, 2017

LUXURIOUS RESORT HOTEL

AS SEEN ON

NBC FOX NEWS abc CNN USA TODAY

Congratulations! You invited to attend an exclusive LIVE Amazon 4-Day Summit that is coming to Las Vegas. This will truly be a once-in-a-lifetime opportunity.

At this summit you will see how to:

✔ NEGOTIATE with manufacturers, SOURCE products, and take advantage of once-in-a-lifetime business opportunities.

✔ Work with our ELITE TEAM of Online Business Strategists and Professional Amazon Sellers to build your Elite Business on Amazon.

✔ Learn how you can realistically generate $10,000+ revenue on Amazon in the next 30-40 days.

✔ Start a REAL BUSINESS, and create a new source of income.

✔ Have PROFESSIONAL SELLERS ACCOUNT and be prepared to begin selling before you leave our summit.

✔ Creating your business the RIGHT WAY is very hard -- we make it easy and show you what NOT to do.

✔ Reach millions of online shoppers who TRUST the Amazon brand.

✔ SAVE time, money, and effort on shipping and warehousing.

✔ Learn from our experts how to advertise within Amazon's platform your product sales and growth

✔ Learn how to utilize REAL STATISTICS, analytics, and number to make educated, profitable decisions for your business.

✔ Offer your products WORLD-WIDE to the specific people searching for them.

✔ Create YOUR OWN brands and businesses with Prime Global Source's elite training and premium resources.

✔ DON'T GET SHUT DOWN: Learn what to AVOID from our professional team to prevent Amazon closing your account and losing business

You will not want to miss this amazing opportunity!

This exclusive program is limited to the first 500 registrants.

Call Now 909-340-9974

Previous advertising graphic from
FEDERAL TRADE COMMISSION v. AWS, LLC; FBA STORES, LLC; INFO PROS, LLC

After the Bowsers and FBA Stores, etc., settled with the FTC, another settlement—this time for nearly $64 million—was reached with one more member of the Amazing Wealth Systems' alleged "con mob."

In that case, Jeffrey Adams—reportedly following a common industry practice of not using his real name—was *also* banned from selling business opportunities, business coaching and making false earnings claims.

More significant to those who say they were scammed though; Adams' company was barred from using consumers' contact information and actually ordered to dispose of it.

The Moral Lawbreakers

On the FTC Website, there are many more examples of just plain stupid Scammers who blatantly violate the law.[24] Later in this book, I'll introduce you to the specific scam techniques used by some of those alleged multi-million dollar offenders.

For now, though, let's move on to the "Moral Lawbreakers."

The "Moral Lawbreakers" can do just as much damage as the Scammers who break state and federal laws, but they've managed (with paid help from some normal human being, probably) to connect enough brain cells to keep from violating actual laws. They hire lawyers to laser-etch protective 'fine print' into their contracts a micron at a time (in minus-38-point text).

They do some of the same things that were described in the preceding *CNet* article and more, but they get away with it because—again—lawyers.

For some of them though, time's up, thanks to the U.S. Consumer Review Fairness Act of 2016. That law now makes it illegal for a company to "gag" its customers by requiring them—as a condition of doing business—to sign a form contract that forbids or restricts their freedom to review or complain about the company.

The first company to get its hand slapped for allegedly breaking that law was—you guessed it—an outfit separately charged with deceptively marketing yet another "system" to make money on Amazon.com. This time it was—an alleged con mob I briefly told you about earlier—a Minnesota company named Sellers Playbook. (You'll learn more about its operations later, since—according to both federal and state governments—its executives appeared to have "skipped the chapter about complying with federal and state consumer protection laws.")

The moral lawbreakers, meanwhile, are the people (and I use that term loosely) who make up the vast majority of the hurricane-strength wind of junk scams and schemes that you're going to have to battle your way through, step by agonizing step, to get to the truth about this business.

(On the other hand, you could just read the rest of this book and avoid the storm completely.)

The "Moral Lawbreakers" and the law-breaking criminals are actually the same kind of people. Morally bankrupt. They know they're lying to you and they simply don't care.

I actually have an **audio recording** of a meeting in which one of these scam marketers told another one that they wanted to sell a product that was worth $500. The other Scammer replied immediately, "Okay, so we charge $5,000 for it." And—incredibly—they did, selling it successfully for years at 10 times what its creator thought it was worth.

That's a true story and sadly, only one of a great many.

People who lie and cheat for a living *usually* consider themselves smarter than the average person. They think people are *idiots* for working hard to accomplish something real. They get together, congratulate each other, and laugh about how they fooled good people into giving up their money for nothing. They call their victims "*sheeple*" and they think it's funny.

The truth is, they're *not* as smart as they think they are. Not by a long shot.

People who always have to lie and cheat their way through a business, in order to make money, simply *aren't smart enough* to build a *legitimate* business and make money honestly. That takes hard work and careful thought, which is something these people either don't know how to do, or don't care to do. That's a fact, and these idiots don't understand that.

Sometimes, with the younger ones that you see drooling buzzwords all over YouTube, it may not be entirely their fault. Some of them may be perfectly intelligent people, but they're *trained* by older, morally bankrupt mercenaries who indoctrinate them into the belief that lying and cheating is the only way to win.

Again, sad but true.

Whether they're corrupt trainers or junior con artists, I don't get angry with them anymore. I used to become infuriated, but in my more than 25 years of experience in online business—often fighting against these people and working to expose them—I've learned something valuable.

No matter how much money they make and how much they get away with, I'm convinced that *Karma* is a screaming banshee on wheels with 40-inch rims, and *never forgets* anything. I believe that these people *will* get "theirs," at some point in their lives, and it'll *hurt*.

Though the reasons behind it may differ, others seem to agree with that prediction of future doom.

Maria Konnikova, author of the 2016 book, *The Confidence Game*, says these con artists often become scam victims themselves, because their inflated sense of self-importance makes them think they're immune to such things.

So while the Scammers still disgust me, most of the time these days I just feel sorry for them in their ignorance, because of the really nasty payback I know they have coming.

The Ignorant Scammers

Ever hear of an affiliate program? So have lots of other people and many of those people have been fooled into thinking you can make money with them.

You really can't; or at least nowhere near as much as they claim.

When you're an affiliate, you market an information or physical product for someone else. Then you send potential customers *to* that someone else. That someone *else* makes the sale.

As an affiliate, you receive a *commission* (a small percentage) often based on the *profit* (not the gross amount) of the sale.

So the affiliate generally earns a *small piece* of the *profit* from sales they send to some other place.

Here's the catch: These days, affiliates have to do just as much marketing work to send their prospects to someone else, as they would be doing if they simply sold their own product themselves. If they sold a product themselves, they could keep *all* the profit!

In short, most affiliate marketing is unrealistic, but almost all of the Scammers out there, both big and small, have affiliate programs.

They sucker their own affiliates just like they sucker everybody else.

So in some cases, there will be affiliates who prance and preen and regurgitate the "pre-written outhouse cookies" the Scammers provided to them, without even checking to see if the program they're pushing is real or a scam!

There's dumb, and there's dumber.

In most cases, though, the affiliates you see pushing e-commerce junk out there are just as morally bankrupt and complicit as all the other future karma-targets in this business.

So, that's a basic description of the three types of "Grifters" in this business; a.k.a. (also known as) confidence men and women, con artists, or Scammers.

They blanket the internet like grains of sand on a beach.

You might find that all-encompassing statement hard to believe. You may think that it's impossible for there to be so many of these Scammers.

That's exactly what the Scammers are counting on.

3 THE MARK

> "I'm a confidence man. I earn people's trust and then I exploit that trust to get whatever I want."
>
> -- Actor Giovanni Ribisi as character
> Pete Murphy, a.k.a. Marius Josipovic,
> in the TV drama series *Sneaky Pete*

In con games, "The Mark" is the target of the scam.

Your name might be Clarence or Matilda, but to the Scammers, it's "Mark," as in target.

Other traditional words for the Mark in a con game (scam) are sucker, stooge, mugu, rube, or gull. None of them sound very pleasant, do they? Of course not. During hunting season—as any deer knows—being a target is *never* pleasant.

For "home-based online business info marketers," hunting season is 365 days a year. The first rule to avoid becoming one of their Marks is to remember that you're always "in season," so you need to carefully choose to whom you'll listen and *exactly* what they say. (Hey, it's not paranoia if they really *are* out to get you, right?)

Nobody wants to be a Mark. Nobody wants to be lied to or cheated.

But, unless they've learned the warning signs, almost everybody who tries to get into home-based business *does* get lied to and cheated.

Why?

Partly because, once the Scammers get a grip on them—they are *willing* to be lied to and cheated.

This is very important to understand: A scam cannot possibly work, unless the Marks are—often on a subconscious level—*willing*. Willing to accept lies. Willing to allow to themselves to be cheated.

This isn't some new concept that just popped up with the internet. Scammers' con games are very sophisticated and have been based on the same psychological factors for *tens of thousands* of years. It's been going on since the first "Stone Ager" fooled his neighbor into trading a sharp rock for a broken stick—hardly a mutually beneficial exchange.

And it's been refined over and over again ever since.

As Scammers have honed their craft over the centuries, confidence games (scams) have become a topic of interest to social researchers, some of whom say that many con artists believe their Marks actually deserve to be scammed,[25] because of common human vulnerabilities like greed, jealousy, laziness and more.

These researchers claim that Scammers have learned to exploit these flaws (hiding their contempt for their Marks as they do it), in order to get their Marks to make critical mistakes. In short, everyone has these vulnerabilities, and con artists will always exploit them.

Some terminologies:

GREED

Some social science investigators say, "greed is the root of a common desire to 'get something for nothing,'" referring to that phrase as a "shorthand expression of a Mark's belief that too-good-to-be-true gains are realistic."[26]

As much as we all hate to admit it, we're all flawed human beings and we all experience greed at some point or another. The Scammers will promise that they'll show you how to make amazing amounts of money, and we *want* that money. We can't help it.

JEALOUSY

Again, *we're human.* It's very difficult to avoid feeling somewhat jealous of others who seem to have so much more in life than we do. *We want that money and success as well.* And Scammers *know* that.

From email campaigns to YouTube videos, blogs and social media all the way up to those three-ring convention-hall buffoonery festivals, the con artists will hammer you over the head with endless examples of how much money *other* people are making.

They'll show you digitally edited bank statements, tell fake stories and create fake testimonials.

When you see these things, try this: pretend that you're a reporter, generations of whom have been trained to value professional skepticism to avoid embarrassment or worse. There's an old expression that keeps reporters on their toes; "If your mother says she loves you, check it out." It's a useful phrase to remember.

Bogus testimonials take many forms, but the "high-quality" ones have at least two things in common:

They tell stories of people who've started a small home-based online business and have made a lot of money quickly on the internet, starting out with little to no experience.

They sound legitimate and seem like true stories.

In reality, they are big fat lies, as was reportedly part of the basis of a Federal Trade Commission lawsuit against four Utah companies who collectively called themselves Fat Giraffe Marketing.

The FTC stated, "In Fat Giraffe's marketing ads, truth was the endangered species."[27]

According to federal investigators, Fat Giraffe, which "sold its purported moneymaking opportunity to consumers nationwide (across the U.S.), claimed "people could rake in cash from the comfort of their homes by simply posting advertising links on websites." The problem, the FTC said, was that "both the success stories and the testimonials were false."

Here's just one example of a Fat Giraffe advertising whopper; a "news story" that looked like it had been reported by no less than five major mainstream news organizations:

Some people might refer to the preceding Fat Giraffe ad as an example of "fake news," but whatever you call it, it's the type of thing that can be initially verified or debunked by going to the "endorsers" web sites (in this case, NBC, ABC, USA TODAY, etc.) and searching for the mom's name and other phrases from the article. (Just remember that mantra about "checking out" a mother's love.)

Sometimes the fake testimonials are face-to-face, lending an even louder ring of truth to claims of success, as Scammers parade their own *employees*—masquerading as successful protégés—onto convention hall stages.

According to one of the scam victims I interviewed, that's just what he believed happened in Texas a few years ago, when a company (that's still in business), skillfully used lengthy testimonials to sell a series of expensive workshops. That scam victim said,

"It was one individual who spoke for an hour and a half, maybe two hours. Lots of testimony about his personal life, how he was in dead-end jobs and that he got into this and it changed his life. And, you know...now he's able to afford all the things (he) could never afford before."

Have you ever experienced people lying to your face? If the lie is convincing enough, it's easy to believe, so how can you avoid getting trapped by those convincing lies?

First, don't let yourself be rushed into buying anything you cannot comfortably afford (more on that later). Then, as you think about the opportunity being offered to you, once again consider the use of that motto about double-checking a "mother's love."

LAZINESS, GULLIBILITY AND DESPERATION

Even the most hard-working people fall victim to the promise of quick, easy money. After all, why work hard for something when it can actually be quick and easy? It's a no-brainer!

The lies surrounding quick and easy riches that these con artists tell are so carefully crafted, fine-tuned and well-presented that even the most steadfast people, who understand hard work, fall victim to them.

Long-time fraudsters, though, are so jaded that they view what most people would consider understandable errors in judgment, as signs of gullibility.[28]

Again, some social researchers say that gullibility reflects the con artist's beliefs that Marks are "suckers" and fools for entering costly voluntary exchanges.

Their heartlessness becomes quite evident when they're able to successfully dump a scam on people who are frantically trying to replace lost income or who—for whatever reason—are desperate to make ends meet.

If that describes you, please remember that if you're reading this, it means that desperation hasn't robbed you of your brain, your patience and your capacity for critical thinking. Right now, in fact, you're gaining valuable knowledge about "how they're gonna come at you" and knowledge really is power.

The Scammers' next big tactic is a concept called Suspension of Disbelief. The phrase first came into existence in 1817, and writers often rely upon the technique to craft books and movies that involve unrealistic storylines.

Here's what Wikipedia[29] has to say about it:

> The term suspension of disbelief has been defined as a willingness to suspend one's critical faculties and believe something surreal. The term was coined in 1817 by the poet and aesthetic philosopher Samuel Taylor Coleridge, who suggested that if a writer could infuse a "human interest and a semblance of truth" into a fantastic tale, the reader would suspend judgment concerning the implausibility of the narrative.

In other words, the better the storyteller, the more a person is willing to believe the story even if it goes against their better judgment.

Suspension of Disbelief combines really well with the 1945 Alexandre Koyre quote; "The mob believes everything it is told, provided only that it be repeated over and over."

Combine these strongly emotional concepts (Suspension of Disbelief and Koyre's statement) with the vast Festival of Leaping

Ninnies that we call the internet, and you have the *perfect conditions* for a "Scam Storm."

When we're kids, we believe in Santa Claus. When we grow up, we find out he's not real, but deep down we still want to believe. Scammers understand that kind of deep-rooted human desire and know exactly how to tap into it.

To recap, from the minute you start exploring this business, you are a Mark. A Mark isn't stupid or ignorant. A Mark is simply hammered with lies and propaganda so often and so convincingly that he or she starts to believe the lies and propaganda.

If you've been scammed in this business, welcome to the Club-of-All-Of-the-Rest-of-Us, because it's happened to me too, long ago.

If you don't *think* you've been *scammed* but aren't *certain*...you *have* been.

If you haven't been scammed at all (meaning you haven't spent a cent on one of these "home-based business opportunities" yet), please finish this book before you even dare to breathe again, because they may be after you right now.

(Okay, you should breathe, but don't do it too loudly. You don't want them to find you!)

By the way... if you *have* been scammed, *don't blame yourself*, because these people are extremely good at what they do. They know all of the right psychological buttons to push. They ask you questions, listen to your answers, and tailor their pitches to exactly what they know you want to hear.

I've physically stood on telemarketing sales floors owned by these people and listened to their pitches myself.

I've heard them promise easy riches, I've heard them tell their Marks that they could own the specific boat or house or car they want within a few months, pay for their kids' college tuition, travel the world and so much more that the scam telemarketers pick up from phone conversations with their Marks.

When they know they're talking to someone who's susceptible to bullying, I've even heard them yell at people, call them *stupid*, and tell them that if they don't fork over the money *right now*, they're idiots and will regret it for the rest of their lives.

So, while a Mark has to be willing to some degree, it's important to remember that these people have absolutely no problem telling you flat-out lies or behaving like bullies in order to make a sale.

Again, if you've been scammed, don't beat yourself up over it. Almost everyone who's tried to start a work-from-home business has been scammed to one degree or another.

What matters now, is that you're "armoring up." Going forward, your decisions about starting an online business will be *informed* decisions and *that* will be one of your best defenses against people who couldn't care less about the truth.

4 THE ROPERS

In a con game, there can be many players, working together in what social researchers call a "con mob."

In con-game terminology, "the Roper" is the member of the con mob who physically finds the Marks to bring to the scam.

In the real world (versus the virtual world), Ropers are used in one-on-one cons, in which the Scammers are pulling off a one-time con against a single specific Mark.

In a case like that, a Roper could be someone as simple as the guy who gets you to try the rigged, ring toss game at a carnival, or the guy who pulls you into a crooked card game, or leads you to a Scammer who's selling land that doesn't exist.

The Roper's job is to identify likely Marks, make first contact with them, and set them up to meet the "Grifter" (a.k.a. Scammer or con artist).

In the older work-from-home "business opportunities" (that went after large numbers of people at once), there was no need for a human "Roper."

Starting in the early 1920's, those fake opportunities were advertised in newspapers and magazines. Because those home-business opportunity scams were mass scams, not one-on-one cons, the newspaper and magazine ads themselves were the Ropes, in this example:

GET PAID FOR MAILING OUR SPECIAL LETTERS FROM HOME
POTENTIAL EARNINGS OF UP TO $5000 OR MORE WEEKLY!
FREE POSTAGE, FREE CIRCULARS, FREE ENVELOPES.
Pay Checks Mailed Every Tuesday.
Don't Get Left Out! Give us a try & receive a check in as little as ten days!

Dear Friend,
Would you like to earn $2,900 to $5,000 each and every week from the comfort of your home? How about MORE than $5,000 a week? Would that help you catch up with your bills, and allow you to relax while enjoying the finer things in life? If you answer is yes, then this is the perfect opportunity for you. We are presently in the midst of hiring home workers for our busy season, and when we say busy, we do mean BUSY. We desperately need at least 250 home workers each week to stuff and mail out our special advertising letters. We have so much work on hand, that we're paying home workers $10.00 for each letter stuffed and returned to us as per instructions. That's right, $10 EACH, the highest rate in the business.

Sample ad for an "Envelope Stuffing Scheme." Graphic from FTC

Then, the internet came along, and that fast-paced digital world changed the way cons were executed. While the core purpose of the swindles hadn't changed, the con artists came up with "new spins on old scams."

As the old newspaper and magazine advertising for work-from-home-scams melted away in favor of the much easier online promotion of "make money from home" scams, the human Ropers re-appeared in force and multiplied like rabbits on an island that only rabbits live on.

In the early days of the world wide web, the cyber con artists focused their advertising and other recruitment efforts on scams like those involving greeting card sales business opportunities, memberships on websites offering "money making secrets," vending machine businesses, jewelry sales displays, mortgage schemes, coffee display rack rip-offs and—of course—envelope stuffing.

A few years later, with the growth of e-commerce, the Scammers evolved again. They began promoting "information marketing," (basically selling people on the idea that they can profit from selling people repetitive or practically useless information) and developing elaborate systems designed to show consumers how to make a lot of money with various other strategies, including the Scammers' plans for people selling products on sites like Amazon.com.

In the ever-growing world of e-commerce—as many recent multi-million dollar FTC busts show us—that's still going on.

If you want to see what Ropers look like today, just go to Google or YouTube and type "make money from home."

There are *thousands* upon *thousands* of them.

If you've been looking into this business, you've probably already watched a steady stream of Ropers parade across your computer screen. If you keep looking, it might be time to get some popcorn, because it's quite a show.

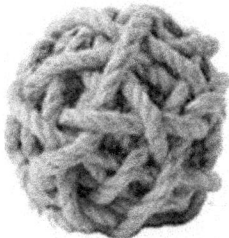

One of the biggest fraud threats to consumers today is that those Ropers in the digital world are invisibly cross-connected. They've tangled themselves into the proverbial Gordian knot.

A Gordian knot is a knot so complex that the ends can't be found, so it's nearly impossible to unravel the knot.

When it comes to Ropers, they're connected to other members of con mobs and they're *everywhere*, in a massive, hidden network with one purpose: separating you from your money.

One good example of that secret entanglement was a U.S. District Court case for the Central District of California, in which the FTC sued four companies based in Delaware, Nevada and the United Kingdom, for allegedly defrauding consumers out of millions of dollars. Some of those consumers reportedly paid more than $50,000 each—in exchange for a promise of individual coaching on how to run an online business.[30]

The "Gordian" way the alleged Scammers promoted their business was to entangle themselves with their own Marks by actually recruiting them into the scam. Here's a look at how they did it from court papers:

IN THE UNITED STATES DISTRICT COURT
FOR THE CENTRAL DISTRICT OF CALIFORNIA

Federal Trade Commission,	**Filed Under Seal**
Plaintiff,	
	No. __2__ :18-CV-__729__-JAK-MRWx
vs.	COMPLAINT FOR PERMANENT INJUNCTION AND OTHER EQUITABLE RELIEF
Digital Altitude LLC, a Delaware limited liability company, Digital Altitude Limited, a United Kingdom company, Aspire Processing LLC, a Nevada limited liability company, Aspire Processing Limited, a United Kingdom company,	

Graphics from FTC vs. Digital Altitude, LLC, Aspire Processing, LLC, US District Court for Central District of California

DEFENDANTS' BUSINESS PRACTICES

31.   Since at least 2015, Defendants have marketed and sold purported money-making opportunities to consumers throughout the United States and abroad. Defendants advertise their purported money-making program extensively through online webpages and social media platforms, including Facebook and Instagram. Once consumers join, Defendants encourage them to add to the marketing effort by placing their own advertisements online, on social media platforms, and otherwise. Defendants make their own advertising copy, branded images, and other marketing materials available to consumers for this purpose, and direct consumers to use these materials in the consumers' marketing efforts. A substantial number of consumers have created marketing websites of their own, posted YouTube videos, and/or placed advertisements and marketing posts of their own on social media, all touting Defendants' program.

They're just Affiliates

If Ropers get former Marks to promote their scams, they're turning them into *affiliates*, a role I wrote about earlier.

But in the *online* work-from-home space, *Ropers* can be affiliates as well.

Both affiliates and Ropers in these cases are like the carnival barkers I've mentioned. It's worth repeating that these are the ones who point you to the games you can't win. They're the cheap suits with the plastic grins who offer to sell you the Brooklyn Bridge, or the shady characters that tap you on the shoulder in a bar and invite you to the rigged poker game. And again—they're *everywhere*.

This is the doorway to the dark side. It's the beginning of all the woeful things that will happen to you if you allow yourself to believe the fairy tales they spin in cyberspace; which is what Roping is all about.

As mentioned, when affiliates rope you into the beginning of an elaborate scam, they get a kickback in the form of a small commission from the Scammers.

Now, some of these affiliates—possibly those in the Digital Altitude case—don't know that what they're doing to you is disgustingly wrong.

That case is a good example of another trap for the unwary.

Here's one more:

According to the FBI, "Some web-based international companies are advertising for affiliate opportunities, offering individuals the chance to sell high-end electronic items, such as plasma television sets and home theater systems, at significantly reduced prices.

The affiliates are instructed to offer the merchandise on well-known Internet auction sites. The affiliates will accept the payments, and pay the company, typically by means of wire transfer. The (bogus) company is then supposed to drop ship the merchandise directly to the buyer, thus eliminating the need for the affiliate to stock or warehouse merchandise. The merchandise never ships, which often prompts the buyers to take legal action against the affiliates, who in essence are victims themselves."[31]

So, some of the affiliates (Ropers) have themselves been roped into doing what they're doing. These are often just people who wanted to start a business themselves; moms and dads, college students, people who are underpaid in their jobs, some who are out of work and desperate for money, and many more I've mentioned at the beginning of this book.

Then, over time, some of them—particularly those who have a

moral compass pointed due south—are fooled into thinking that what they do is acceptable behavior in business. They're led to believe that suckering people into the sheep-shearing pen for a good old-fashioned fleecing is—in the business world--*within acceptable limits.*

But most of these affiliates, know—from the beginning—that what they're doing is wrong.

And those who do know and still do it…simply don't care.

In a Harvard Gazette interview[32] with Psychologist Maria Konnikova, we can begin to understand the reasons for that coldhearted attitude. Konnikova said the majority of con artists are narcissists.

According to the Mayo Clinic, that's a description of people who have an inflated sense of their own importance, a deep need for excessive attention and admiration…and a lack of empathy for others.[33]

Konnikova also claims that these Scammers have a sense of entitlement, which helps them justify, to themselves and to others, the financial destruction they inflict on their victims' lives.

It isn't surprising then, that the affiliates who have the mindset of a swindler will always try to sell you whatever pays them *the highest commissions*, regardless of whether it's a good product.

Real products pay lower commissions. Because *real products* actually have development and maintenance costs, they can't afford to pay massive commissions to affiliates.

Scam products *don't* have those costs and because those who sell them eventually charge you a *lot* more money for them, they *can* afford to pay massive commissions to affiliates.

In that twisted way of looking at things, the affiliates will always think it makes more sense for them to ignore the good products and information they *could* be promoting and instead, hammer you with the crap that feeds their own wallets the most cash. (Which, of course, comes out of your wallet.)

Since affiliates are paid to sell *whatever they can*, they try to push you into as many scams as they can. One thing always leads to another, which leads to another and another, and so on.

Sharon, one of the people I interviewed, learned that lesson the hard way. She never dreamed that once she gave out her contact information—to just one affiliate—that she would be bombarded with promotional emails. Those emails became a clue that something wasn't right.

Sharon told me, "I was on his email list for something that I got from him. It seemed like every week he was sending in his email newsletter thing, a different opportunity... after a little while, I realized, 'Wait a minute, if this is making him so much money, he's either really, really greedy, or these things aren't working the way that they're supposed to work, because otherwise, you wouldn't be needing something new every week.'"

The trash they push on you is often conflicting and is always confusing, and never ends.

That unconscionable willingness to connect with every junk affiliate program they can find and market whatever makes them the most money--no matter what it is—creates the enormous, concealed Gordian knot of the Roper world.

So many of these Ropers are just ignorant, greedy people who have no understanding of how to build a real business, so they take what they think is the easy way out. They climb on board the "Amazing-Affiliate-Cheat-Train" and gleefully blow the air horn all the way down the track, through your computer screen and into your bank account.

What most of them *don't* realize, though, is that in a relatively short period of time, once their victims start to realize what's happened and start to complain about them, they're going to end up with a lot negative feedback online. Their names will turn to mud in 6 months to a year, and they'll self-implode.

When that happens, the most dastardly and resilient of them will simply change to a different online name, slap together a different website, and just keep on drooling the same old river of garbage.

This is why people see so many new names come and go in this business. A lot of them are just the same "Ropers" changing their names and websites once their proverbial kitchens "get too hot."

The Scammers are "Ropers" too

In a disgustingly interesting twist, in the online world the Scammers themselves have also—*in the online world*—become Ropers.

Yes, even the *creators* of all these "Most Amazing Secret Ninja Lifestyle Easy Money Get Rich Quick Doing Stupid Things That Don't Work And We Won't Really Show You Anyway" programs will—at different times in the process of fleecing you out of your money—tell you that you *must* buy into *other* scams.

They scam and they rope. Why? Well…because of the extra money.

What They Look Like

As I said earlier, if you've been looking into online work-from-home business *at all*, you already have an idea of what they look like.

On YouTube and in the videos they promote through their emails:

- Some of them wear suits and ties and try to look like successful business people.

- Some of them hang on a beach or hike through the mountains when they talk to you.

- Some of them prance around as if they're "from the hood" and say "yo"and "check it" a lot.

- Some sit in front of computers and use lots of shiny graphics.

- Some of them drive up in expensive cars, get out, and tell you how they can make you easy money.

- Some lounge in huge mansions and show off pools and expensive art.

And so on.

A perfect example of the use of "McMansions," expensive cars and other luxury items like yachts, comes from Utah's FTC versus Fat Giraffe lawsuit.

You can have all your life wishes if you just apply yourself to this program

Graphic from Federal Trade Commission v. Fat Giraffe Marketing
Group, LLC, et al. al

The preceding photos are taken from the pages of that court case—all of them images of lavish possessions tied together with the caption, "You can have all your life wishes if you just apply yourself to this program."

When he was viewing advertising from another of these alleged Scammers, my Ecommerce Education student Ivan, a veteran of the military, witnessed that exact same ploy.

Ivan told me, "This one guy drives around in a Lamborghini. Yeah, he had, like, this expensive car and he shows up…and he takes off his glasses and says, "Let me teach you how to (confidential description of product). Eventually, towards the end—they will never say it at the beginning—they will say something along the lines of "This is about how you progress. Not everybody gets the same results, *but if you work hard enough, it will happen for you.*"

These things are *visual illusions* based on classic marketing psychology. It's all part of the Rope.

When it comes to suits and ties, you can often tell that the Ropers aren't used wearing them. (They seem more like the type of people who are more comfortable in munching Cheetos in their underwear, sitting in front of a video game in their parents' basements.)

They do the beach and hiking thing to make you *feel* like making loads of money is just a *casual* thing.

They want you to think, "Yeah. Making money is easy. It's as though they're hoping that you'll "Just watch me hiking around some trail with my selfie stick and iPhone, and I'll hand you the universal secrets to amazing money and success and—by the way—I'm really fit and cool and you will be too!"

They do the 'from the hood' imitation with the "yo" and "check it" thing because they think they need to appeal to a younger audience who might have access to their mommy and daddy's credit cards.

They do the "computer and shiny graphics" thing to appeal to people they think are more upscale and can be fleeced for larger amounts of money.

The expensive cars they drive up in are *rented* for the day so they can make their videos. (Yes, really.)

The huge mansions they prance around in are rented for the same reason. (Again, yes, really. There are all kinds of properties you can rent short-term to make videos).

It's all an illusion. For the most part, these people are simply affiliates who make cash in exchange for Roping you and throwing you to the wolves. *Don't forget that.*

What They Sound Like

Don't ever forget, either, that the Scammers script the things they say to you in videos and emails.

As was demonstrated in the FTC versus Digital Altitude court case, most affiliates are just parrots; all the clever-sounding patter they use is *provided* for them by the Scammers themselves. This is a signature aspect of affiliate marketing. The company (a.k.a. the Scam) that runs the affiliate program provides text, images, ad copy and "sales letters" to their Affiliates.

It's important for the affiliates to use that pre-written stuff that they had nothing to do with, because—when the affiliate connects you to the actual scam—it creates a smooth transition.

The Scammers actually *demand* that their Ropers (affiliates) only say and do things created by the Scammers themselves.

Their emails are very carefully based on emotion—the psych factors we talked about earlier.

They will promise you everything you ever wanted. They'll often even make promises of specific amounts of money. These are called "earnest money claims," and unless they have proof that people in their program have actually made those amounts of money, these claims are illegal.

As you might imagine by now, that doesn't matter to them. Hey, a new online identity is just around the corner, right?

Squeezing Isn't Just for Lemons

The Scammers emails will lead you to what they call "squeeze pages." As in, "squeeze you psychologically into a sales funnel in every way they can, until money pops out of your pants."

We'll talk more about "squeeze pages" later. For now, just know that "squeeze pages" are often long and rambling web pages that contain lots of *different* psychological ploys. They're long; because they want to make sure, they catch everybody. To do that, they need to say all the different things that different people need to hear in order to be fooled into buying junk.

Ever notice that some web pages have lots of "Buy It Right Now" links, spaced throughout the content of the page? Next time you have some time to waste, actually read those pages page carefully.

If you do, you'll notice that each time the conversation switches to a different *emotional psych ploy*, there will be a "Buy It Right Now" link just before the *change* in emotional tone.

This "sections" the squeeze page into many separate "commercials," each one aimed at catching people with different emotional weaknesses.

Again, they want to make sure they catch everybody.

When it comes to their *videos*, they'll start out sounding perfectly reasonable, gradually gearing up to the point that they make outrageous promises, while still making them sound reasonable. Some of their presentations are very good. Others—when viewed by those who've been educated about what to watch for—are ridiculously bad.

During my research for this book, I watched a long and boring video by some yutz out there who claims that all you need are 10,000 email addresses to contact, and *everything* will work, to make you lots of money. Amazon, eBay, "private labeling," yadda, yadda, yadda, ad nauseum.

They say that all you need to do is buy that "Amazing System," sit back, and watch the cash roll in.

Um, no.

First, there is *no number of email addresses* that will make any of those things work for a home-based business owner. By themselves, they don't do *anything*.

Second, nothing is easy about starting and building your own business. (But easy sure does sound good!)

These videos will *always* contain plays on emotion as well. Another video sent to me by one of the people I interviewed for this book has a "heart to heart interlude" that goes like this:

> "That dream life you've always wanted is sitting right at your fingertips. Now imagine with me for a moment, what does 'dream life' mean for you? It's different for everybody.
>
> For some, it's Lamborghinis and champagne. Others, it's building schools in Africa. For others it's about being able to spend more time with family and travel the world. And still others, it's simply having enough to feel secure in their finances.
>
> What does it mean for you? Knowing what it means to you is key to having the motivation to accomplish it. We're gonna help you accomplish that dream with our brand new..."

There's more, but it already makes me a little nauseated and I don't have time to run to the bathroom right now. The point is; this kind of BS emotional assault on your wallet is utterly disgusting, blatantly false and even patronizing.

But they *all* do it in one way or another. As soon as a Roper or Scammer—pitching a home-based business--starts talking about your "hopes and dreams," hit the stop button, x-out the page, delete the bookmark. In short, run—as fast as you can—the other way.

The Scarcity Play.

A "scarcity play" is a legitimate form of marketing that is used all over the place for just about everything you can buy. A three-day sale at Macy's is a "scarcity play." A limited time offer at Tire Kingdom is a "scarcity play." Holiday sales are "scarcity plays." You get the idea.

"Scarcity plays" are called "scarcity" because they're always *limited time sales*. Get it before the deadline, or it's no longer on sale. In the legitimate business world described above, that's true.

Ropers and Scammers use them all the time as well, but they *lie* about them. They'll tell you that something is only available until Friday, so you jump in and buy it, and then you realize that they're telling people the very next day that it's on sale *again* and only available until next *Wednesday*.

It's true that legitimate companies will sometimes extend sales, but at some point, *they have to stop*. Scammers never do, they just do things like switch their database of Marks, change their product names, etc.

Before I met them, my students Mike and Sandy ran into a scarcity play that made them realize that the business-building program they were involved in was actually a scam. They were offered a chance to purchase a program that would accelerate their progress and received a follow up email that tipped them off to the inner workings of a fraud.

According to Mike, "They said to us they were shutting it down for possibly for 12 to 18 months and there wouldn't be another opportunity. That was a blatant lie, because two days later they opened it up."

When it comes to Ropers and Scammers, the only thing that's scarce is the *truth*.

Later in this book, I'll provide you with more tips to recognize when you're being "squeezed" and confronted with scarcity plays, because some of them aren't as obvious as you'd think.

For now, there it is; the Ropers get paid to lead you to scams and they don't care what the scams are as long as they make money.

To recap: Ropers are affiliate marketers who cross-connect with as many affiliate programs as they can to make as much money as they can, no matter how badly they hurt you.

Ropers are most often parrots who squawk whatever the Scammers *tell* them to squawk and often know next to nothing about the businesses they promote.

Ropers can be Scammers themselves, and Scammers can be Ropers as well.

It's a huge, hidden Gordian knot, and it's tied around nearly everything you see online related to starting a business from home.

What's the classic solution to untying the Gordian knot?

Cut the rope.

5 THE LONG CON

Now that you've been introduced to some of the key players in an e-commerce or business opportunity work-from-home "con mob," I want you to become familiar with one of this con game's subtypes, called "The Long Con." This is sometimes also referred to as a "Long Game," or a "Big Con."

The terminology used, depends upon who's describing the scam.

There are social researchers who prefer the term "Big Con," because it hints that there are many people and moving parts necessary to pull off such a con. A Big Con can *also* refer to the large economic impact of the con.

A well-known example of the large economic impact of a Long/Big Con includes the scam reportedly pulled off by Wall Street financier Bernie Madoff.[34]

For over a decade—at least—Madoff ran what's called a ponzi scheme,[35] a form of fraud that lures investors with promises of huge profits. The scheme then pays those profits to the earliest investors with funds from more recent investors.

In Madoff's case, when he could no longer pay early investors with fresh investment funds, the whole scam came crashing down, resulting in billions of dollars of investor losses.

In the bogus e-commerce/business opportunity world, there are "Madoff-like" schemes going on all of the time, costing innocent victims hundreds of millions of dollars every year.

Many of these victims are too embarrassed to complain, don't know to whom they should complain, or—because the schemes are complex—don't know how to complain without the help of an undercover investigator who can confirm the existence of a con game.

In the FTC court case against the U.S. and international founders of "My Online Business Education" (MOBE), there were similarities to Madoff's Ponzi scheme in that the only way "investors" could make money was if other "investors" coughed up some of theirs.

An excerpt from that court case[36] explains:

UNITED STATES DISTRICT COURT
MIDDLE DISTRICT OF FLORIDA

2018 JUN -4 AM 11: 20

FEDERAL TRADE COMMISSION,

Plaintiff,

v.

TWELVE U.S. AND INTERNATIONAL
INDIVIDUALS AND COMPANIES

Defendants

Filed Under Seal

Case No. _____

COMPLAINT FOR PERMANENT
INJUNCTION AND OTHER
EQUITABLE RELIEF

4. Defendants eventually reveal, as consumers progress through the steps, that the way to make money through MOBE is by luring other consumers into the MOBE program and earning commissions when these consumers buy the same costly memberships.

In short, like Madoff's scheme, MOBE's alleged scheme and many more scams floating on the internet today, *there is no product or service involved.* Money is only paid to investors when additional investors give their money to the Scammers.

Of course, there are many other e-commerce/business opportunity work-at-home scams that *do* claim to be based upon sales of a product or service—selling products online at Amazon.com for example—and they too, are both long and big.

The length, or duration, of the scheme is elaborately tied to its huge impact.

When it comes to the time-span, here's how Wikipedia describes the "Long Con,"

"A long con is a scam that unfolds over several days or weeks and involves a team of swindlers, as well as props, sets, extras, costumes, and scripted lines. It aims to rob the victim of huge sums of money or valuable things, often by getting him or her to empty out banking accounts and borrow from family members."[37]

One of the many techniques that Scammers use to keep their Marks involved in a Long Con is to keep selling them products that they simply "must have" in order to achieve major success using the *first* program they bought.

That's just one version of the Scammers' use of a Long Con. There are many more, because there's a constant, overriding theme relied upon by "Scam World Grifters" who use these "Long Cons." The theme contains their mantra; their overriding imperative. It's the one thing they require and upon which they base their entire existence.

It's called, *"recurring revenue."*

Now, it's important to understand that in marketing, the idea of recurring revenue is a core principle. Sell your customer a good product, generate loyalty, and they will continue to buy from you. If you buy a good brand of dish soap and it works well, you're likely to buy it again. Because you like the dish soap, you may also purchase laundry detergent from the same brand. In both cases, you use it, run out of it, and you buy it again.

That describes a *legitimate* way of building a source of recurring revenue.

The "Scam World" way is the Frankenstein version, as my student Mark found out after he saw an ad for an e-commerce workshop.

Mark told me, "(They said) 'Come to our free two-hour workshop here in Sugarland' and I thought, 'Okay, I got a couple hours, I'll go check it out.' So, I listened to them speak and they said, 'Now, if you want to come to our three-day workshop, we need $800 today.'"

Mark continued, "In the workshop, they show you an Advanced, a Professional and an Elite program. Their Advanced program was $12,995. Professional program, the price was $16,995. And then their Elite program for $22,995. They would add, BUT, the elite program, look at all the different things that are offered. That's what steered me toward it was the fact that it had all of these added "benefits and bonus programs" and other things added to it. So in my head, I said, 'If you're going to go in, go all in ($22,995)."

Added Mark, "About a month after that, I got a call from them. This person said, 'We've got this one-time offer going on right now it's a special deal. We're providing mentors and coaches for some of our elite members, these people will get on the phone with you on a weekly basis.' And stupid guy that I am, I said, 'Alright, I'd like to have a coach because I really want to move this thing on faster.' So I paid another outrageous sum for this coach ($15,000). **There were three credit cards that I put this $37,000 on.**"

So, there was Mark—having been lured into what now appears to have been a sophisticated, undetectable con—accepting the all-too-common invitation to purchase another scam product that he hoped would make the first product work the way it had been originally promised to work, *without* the addition of another product.

And notice how he was contacted a month later, by "someone" he didn't know? He couldn't have recognized it at the time, but that was a clear clue that he was involved in a Big/Long Con with many moving parts.

Social researchers say, "A Big Con typically requires a diverse set of tasks that no single individual can carry out" and that "Big Cons' 'inside men' are 'highly specialized workers,' who have 'a superb knowledge of psychology to keep the mark under control during the days or weeks' when the mark is induced to use his resources to participate in the game."[38]

Regardless of the techniques they use or how well they're trained, when these evil clowns fool their customers into buying crap on a stick and calling it a shish kabob and then lie to them—in order to further sell them crap on a plate, crap in a bowl and several monthly repeating orders of various crap protein shakes—*that's a problem.*

And that's the Scammers' version of recurring revenue.

It doesn't matter to them that ingesting all that crap will make you sick. The only thing that matters to them is that you keep buying more and more of it.

Nearly everybody in the how-to-make-money-from-home information business is involved in the Scam-World-Long-Con "business model" of recurring revenue. Frankly, it's disgusting.

Whether it's some huckster who tells you that gathering 10,000 email addresses will solve all your problems, or some yapping Chihuahua who calls you and tells you that if you just mortgage your house you can pay it all off in three months, or a "Circus Of Leaping Ninnies" at a convention center or even the largest, most well-known e-commerce service providers in the world, the "Long Con" is at the center of their game and it's all they care about.

Although my student Mark wound up forking over $37,000, that sum included smaller amounts as well as larger amounts.

The fact that he made smaller purchases is significant, because the

"Long Con" always starts small. Something free that leads to something you're required to purchase that isn't too expensive—at least in the view of someone who's expecting to pay *something* in exchange for starting a business.

After the Scammers have convinced you to shell out for the "not too expensive" thing, the next item on the menu will be one of dozens of *little* things that will require a monthly subscription. (Remember the Gordian knot?)

Then, when none of that stuff works for you (which it won't), they'll tell you that it's because you don't have the *premium* "system," and that's another $10,000.

And when *that* doesn't work, they'll tell you (in much nicer terms) that you're just a flaming idiot who can't do anything right, so you need their *"coaching services"* if you're ever going to earn back the $20,000 you've already flushed down their toilet, and that "coaching" is another $15,000.

Here's how parts of that concept worked in the FTC (Federal Trade Commission) court claim against MOBE.[39]

From:

SUMMARY OF CASE, Federal Trade Commission, Plaintiff, v. MOBE Ltd., United States District Court Middle District of Florida

---

3.   Although the initial entry fee for Defendants' 21-Step System is relatively modest—typically $49 or less—as consumers proceed through the steps, they are bombarded with sales pitches for various MOBE membership packages costing thousands of dollars that consumers must buy in order to continue through and complete the 21-Step System.

So let's say you go ahead and purchase one of the Scammers' premium "systems," thinking that you will finally have all of the tools and training to be successful in the Scammers' programs.

Think again.

For Mark, who was trying to learn how to sell products on Amazon.com, an introduction one of the scammer's more expensive training products was like a journey into *The Twilight Zone*.

Mark told me, "It was information overload. They pour so much into your head…that it's difficult to sort it all out. But at the same time, they're very good at what they do and they make it look very user-friendly and very easy to do."

Now, on the off chance that you're able to sort out all of the confusing information you're given, the next hurdle you may face is huge and very common:

Instructions are essential in order for the "system" to work, are often missing.

This major "system" flaw is a little like being given product instructions written in Korean, when you neither speak nor read Korean and there is no way for you to learn enough Korean to make sense of the instructions.

Mark continued, "I was so good at analyzing product. Then my next question was, OK, where do I get the product? I want to find a wholesaler or distributor, so I can actually get my hands on the product. That's information they don't give you. And they give very little help to figure that out."

When my student Mike was also trying to learn how to sell products on Amazon.com—using training and tools he'd purchased from a *different* suspected scammer—he was introduced to a system that involved how to source products from China for resale.

That's when Mike found out that the "very little help" to which Mark referred, was *also* a characteristic of *his* alleged Scammer's "mentors," who, Mike says, not only sat on their thumbs when asked tough questions, but actually became hostile.

Mike says he was a target of their antagonism, when he asked some challenging questions of leaders in the online support community the alleged Scammers had set up—a common psychological ploy used to delay a victims' discovery that they have been scammed.

As a con artist technique, such an online community might actually serve *three purposes* for this alleged scammer, who—as mentioned—is *still* in business, Roping in people with promises that they can learn how to make buckets of money selling products on Amazon.com.

The first psychological purpose is based upon a ploy called, "the Principal of Misdirection."

According to Alexis Conran, co-host of the *BBC The Real Hustle*, "Misdirection is an age-old tactic used by thieves of all kinds. It's why pick pockets snatch wallets when they know we're occupied by an outdoor concert or fireworks display or by reading our phones or books while we commute."

The e-commerce-business-opportunity-work-at-home Scammers use the strategy of "Misdirection" in many different ways.

After their victims have been Roped in and have paid for an expensive "system," Scammers will sometimes use subtle Misdirection by requiring them to learn how to use complex software they hired someone to develop on the cheap.

Often, it takes a lot of time to learn how to use this software and while doing so, there's a good chance the Marks believe it's just part of the training that will lead to learning the rest of a complete system. They may also think that the software is cool—because it often has a lot of "bells and whistles," they haven't seen elsewhere on the internet.

Sometimes—before they've even finished learning how to use the software—the Marks may be asked to pay for an upgrade, in order to take advantage of "must have" improvements.

They don't know that this "bright shiny software object" is actually a Scammer's clever use of the ploy of Misdirection, delaying the day when the Mark learns he or she has been scammed.

After all, there's so much about the "system" that they still have to learn, right? (And so many more products to buy.)

The online community, to which my student Mike belonged, may have also represented a more subtle use of the Misdirection ploy, as well as something even more powerful; a way for the alleged Scammers to benefit from two related weapons in the arsenal of con artistry; tactics called "Social proof" and "Social Compliance."

According to BBC host Conran, Social Proof refers to how "we constantly look to others around us for clues as to how to behave...That's a very, very powerful thing because as a hustler, I know that all I have to do is manipulate your environment to get you to behave the way I want you to."[40]

In Mike's case, the alleged Scammers offered "badges" to members of the community who were active and helpful to others as they learned how to use the "systems" they had purchased.

Mike and his wife and business partner Sandy actually earned a badge before they began suspecting that they'd been scammed.

Mike said, "We were really trying to help people that were in the same situation we were. So part of our driving force was not only to help ourselves, but to try to help others, to try to maintain some, you know, positivity within this program. But then it comes to the point where when you ask a mentor a question, and they're rude to you, you need to put that out in the community or such as tariffs, when the Chinese tariffs really started getting going, boy I'll tell you that was a subject they shut down real fast."

Sandy's experience was a mirror image of Mike's.

She said, "I would ask a lot of questions. And I would get such rebuttal because I would ask so many questions, because it was just things weren't jiving, something wasn't right. And so I would ask questions, I go in the community and ask, and they shut me down."

What Mike and Sandy interpreted as rude behavior may have actually been calculated, using the next con artistry maneuver, Social Compliance, which, according to *The Real Hustle* host Conran, refers to "how we respond to people in authority and to badges and uniforms."

Host Conran added, "While this is essential to the functioning of our society — it's why the sight of a police car can make drivers immediately slow down — but it also leaves us vulnerable to people like Bernie Madoff who rely on the appearance of competence and expertise to disguise what they're really doing."

In Mike and Sandy's case, they were dealing with alleged Scammers who *first* delivered what seemed like *authoritative claims* that using their systems would result in success selling products on Amazon.

After Roping in their victims with that claim, the alleged Scammers may have:

1. Misdirected them by herding them together in an online community,

2. Relied on Social Proof by encouraging them to earn "badges" through their helpful "busyness," thus demonstrating how to behave in order to gain status in the community and

3. Enforced Socially Compliant behavior through authoritarian online censorship of comments by "rebels" who asked reasonable questions and might be on the verge of voicing their suspicions that everyone was being taken to the cleaners.

Although the alleged Scammers' possible tactics backfired when it came to forcing Mike and Sandy to return to more "Socially Compliant" behavior, there are other "fish in the sea," right?

There sure are and none of those future victims yet know that all of the "systems" offered by the Scammers are based on half-baked, incomplete representations of business concepts that aren't viable for home-based business owners anyway.

You never have a chance.

Remember that I said near the beginning of this book that these people think you're stupid and can't ever learn to run a real business anyway, so in their greedy little minds, why should they bother stepping up to the plate and actually putting in the time and effort to try to teach you something that's viable?

Much easier, for them to just feed you information that they know is useless (information that is really cheap for them to create) and keep you dangling in the barbed-wire fence until your cash bleeds out.

"The Long Con" never ends until you run out of money.

6 THE SHILL

Google's dictionary defines a "shill" as follows:

---

shill
/SHil/

noun
1.
an accomplice of a hawker, gambler, or swindler who acts as an enthusiastic customer to entice or encourage others.

verb
1.
act or work as a shill.

In a con game, "The Shill" is a willing accomplice of the Scammer. This is someone who pretends to be a complete outsider just like you—someone who got involved in whatever the Scammer is pitching. This Shill's key role is to claim to have made all kinds of money from the Scammer's coaching program, business opportunity or work-from-home scheme.

Examples are everywhere. Before I met some of my students,

many of them had seen Shills but didn't know they were Shills. Why not? One reason; people who are true experts at the "craft" of deliberate Shilling are very convincing.

According to my student Sandy, "I ran across this video about how this 23-year-old woman went from making zero to $50,000 a month. That was the first thing that really got my interest."

During my interview with my student Mark, he told me about testimonials offered on stage during a live event. According to Mark, "During the first couple hours (it was) about the business. And then toward the end of that day, it was just more testimonials from the people about how great their lives have been since they've gotten into all this stuff."

The Shill is usually working for or is paid in some way by the Scammer.

In emails, videos and web pages, you'll often see these Shills giving "testimonials." They'll tell you how their lives have completely changed, how much money they've made and how successful they are. *Often, their names and pictures are as phony as their stories.*

A perfect example of that is the following FTC court case against an astounding number of 24 Defendants who—according to the FTC—used fake "rags-to-riches' stories—complete with fraudulently identified photos—in order to market a dishonest work-from-home scheme. Here are some of the details:

FTC Press Release (February 24, 2014):[41]

FTC Halts Multi-Million Dollar Work-From-Home Business Coaching Scheme

Consumers Lost Thousands of Dollars Each, After Being Told They Could Earn Income Through Online Businesses At the Federal Trade Commission's request, a federal court entered a temporary restraining order halting a deceptive work-from-home scheme that conned millions of dollars from consumers by falsely telling them they could easily earn thousands of dollars a month by purchasing bogus business coaching services and establishing their own internet businesses. According to the FTC, consumers who bought into the scheme lost thousands – sometimes tens of thousands – of dollars each, most of it through racking up huge credit card charges at the defendants' urging.

The U.S. District Court for the District of Utah froze the assets of the defendants, who did business under a variety of names, including Essent Media, LLC, Net Training, LLC, Utah-based YES International, Coaching Department, and Apply Knowledge, and appointed a temporary receiver to take control of the operations, pending the outcome of a preliminary injunction hearing set for March 20, 2014. The FTC seeks to put a permanent stop to the operations and return money to consumers.

"This case halts a massive scam that bilked consumers out of millions for useless work-at-home kits and business coaching services," said Jessica Rich, Director of the Bureau of Consumer Protection. "The defendants duped consumers into thinking they could earn thousands working from home. Protecting consumers from such pernicious schemes remains a top priority."

In the court case against those 24 Defendants (individuals and their companies) the FTC said that the Defendants' websites featured many stories about people who bought the defendants services, as in the case of an ad featuring a testimonial from a so-called "Sally Brown:"[42]

> My name is Sally Brown, and let me tell you, I used to work hard... Really hard... And like millions of other Americans... While hardly getting by, living from pay check to pay check.
>
> I got divorced at a very young age and I was left with having to find a new place to live with my 6 year old daughter. I moved to New Jersey for a fresh start on life which was not easy. I had to work two jobs waitressing and some freelance work on the side just to pay bills.
>
> No matter how hard I worked my bank balance was always at zero at the end of each month, and my credit cards kept accumulating more and more debt. I hated my jobs, my bosses and the debt.
>
> **The Chilling Day That Changed My Life...**
>
> I remember the exact day: It was June 17th, and I got laid off from my full time job, the one that was paying the majority of bills. It was a few days before my little girl's birthday and I was supposed to buy Shannon the birthday presents she had been hoping for. But all of a sudden, I could no longer afford gifts. I didn't even know how I could get enough money together to pay the rent, let alone the food for

According to the FTC's court claim, "The Defendants' website tells how 'Sally' went from being a struggling single mother, to earning thousands of dollars a month working just a few hours a day from home, by posting affiliate links online..." The agency went on to state, "The Defendants' website claims that consumers who post links using the (Defendants' system) can work from home an hour and a half a day, five days a week, and earn $97,500 a year... These representations are false or unsubstantiated."

The FTC court claim further stated, "Other Work-At-Home-Kit Websites used by Defendants make similar misrepresentations" and that visitors to some of those other websites encountered a screen with yet another "rags-to-riches" story, except on those websites, "Sally" was now named "Jessica."

How would you like an easy, proven, and guaranteed way to make extra money from home in your spare time? If you answered yes then this will be the most exciting message that you'll ever read!

And here's why: My name is Jessica Bradley and let me tell you, I used to work hard , really hard and, like millions of other Americans, while hardly getting by, living from pay check to pay check.

I got divorced at a very young age and I was left with having to find a new place to live with my 2 years old daughter.

I moved to Ohio for a fresh start on life which was not easy. I had to work two jobs waitressing and some office work on the side just to pay bills. No matter how hard I worked my bank balance was always at zero at the end of each month, and my credit cards kept accumulating more and more debt. I hated my jobs, my bosses and the debt.

THE CHILLING DAY THAT CHANGED MY LIFE...

I remember the exact day: It was May 19th, and I got laid off from my full time job, the one that was paying the majority of bills. It was a few days before my little girl's birthday and I was supposed to buy Eleena the birthday presents she had been hoping for.

But all of a sudden, I could no longer afford gifts. I didn't even know how I could get enough money together to pay the rent, let alone the food for us.

Here's where the story about this case becomes a tale of cold-hearted cunning.

According to the FTC complaint, "Even the pictures are misleading. The photo of Jessica Bradley from the (Defendants' website) is actually a photo titled 'Woman Posing with Baby Girl' available from a stock photo agency."

The FTC offered the following "menu" of stock photo purchase options as proof that the image of "Jessica" was available for use by anyone with a credit card:

But the alleged Scammers didn't stop there. In addition to reportedly showcasing a person who represented some of the most vulnerable among us—a careworn, impoverished single mother—the Defendants' also reportedly chose to tell a phony story about a representative of another sometimes disadvantaged group; people who are unfamiliar with how to use computer technology.

Look at this depiction that—once again—features a fake testimonial matched to a stock photo:

In a continuation of its press release about the case against the 24 Defendants, the FTC also stated: "The defendants' scheme had three inter-connected phases. In the first phase, the defendants used deceptive emails and websites to induce consumers to purchase relatively inexpensive work-at-home kits. They sold these kits, which typically cost from $37 to $99, with claims such as:

> "*If You Can Spare 60 Minutes A Day, We Can Offer You a Certified, Proven And Guaranteed Home Job To Make $379/Day From Home!*"
>
> "*Important: Read my full report now as only 15 people are accepted into this program per city at any given time . . . because of the personal support given to each new member to ensure everyone's quick financial success. Don't hesitate . . . this page is taken down (literally) when the limit is reached, so read on . . .*"

The FTC continued:

But instead of showing consumers how to earn this income, the websites tried to sell them more products or services. In the second phase of their scheme, the defendants promised consumers that they would earn thousands of dollars a month using defendants' coaching program to assist them in establishing their own online businesses. The defendants also encouraged consumers to put the entire cost of the program, generally from $3,000 to $12,000, on their credit card, claiming they would be able to pay it off within a few months. In the third phase of their scheme, the defendants pretended to provide consumers with the promised "coaching" services, while pitching yet additional costly add-on services such as business formation, website design, website development, accounting and tax filing services, and drop-shipping services, none of which proved helpful.

According to the FTC, most people who bought the defendants' services did not get a functional online business, earned little or no money, and ended up heavily in debt.

The FTC has alleged that the defendants violated the FTC Act by misrepresenting likely earnings and the nature of their services and also violated the FTC's Telemarketing Sales Rule by misrepresenting material aspects of their investment opportunities."

Because of taking these alleged villains to court, the FTC was able to send refund checks to thousands of people who purchased "business coaching services" from the Defendants, but it took several years to reach a court ordered settlement and the amount of each check averaged only $169.

More importantly for the future, the Defendants' were banned from "selling business coaching programs and investment opportunities, from credit card laundering and telemarketing" and "from profiting from consumers' personal information collected as part of the challenged practices, and failing to dispose of it properly."[43]

In contrast to the counterfeit, two-dimensional "testimonials" referred to in the preceding court case, what I call the "Nine Ring Circuses," advertised as hotel convention room "workshops." Attendees actually hear from live people who are paraded up to the microphone at psychologically strategic times in order to hype you up and emotionally drive you closer to jumping off whatever cliff they're herding you toward.

Granted, *it's true* that testimonials from real satisfied customers are often displayed by reputable companies. Those endorsements are genuine, and they're valuable marketing tools.

But notice the word reputable. We're not talking about reputable companies here.

The *scam* companies are in business *specifically to mislead you* into buying as much useless junk as they can cram down your emotionally choked-up throat. That means they have no problem lying to you, so most of the time, the testimonials come from paid Shills or from their own employees, who are pretending to be a random member of the crowd.

But *sometimes*, the Shill is someone *real* who doesn't know that he or she is shilling. The Scammers will invite *newer* members of their "Amazing Money-Making Cash Machines" to give testimonials for them.

These newer members haven't had time to realize how badly they've been screwed over and they're thrilled to be invited up on stage in front of the crowd, so they play along.

They're not alone.

Social researchers refer to these "innocent" members of a con-mob as "enablers," versus "participants." They say that "history has shown over and over again that …enablers do not always understand that their work furthered unlawful schemes."[44]

Sometimes, the Scammers will offer extra bonuses and benefits to those newer members in exchange for glowing testimonials, but not always.

When my students Mike and Sandy were involved in what they later learned was a scam business opportunity program, they joined an online group set up for members to support each other as they progressed through learning how to import products from China and sell them on Amazon.com.

Mike and Sandy said they actually expressed support for the program's leaders during their interactions with others in the online group, until they started learning things that made them suspicious.

As Mike tells it, "We were trying to help others believe what we were starting to disbelieve. We tried to remain positive for our own well-being and hoping to God that this was not what was really happening… (but) our gut was right. And you know, I mean, as far as exactly when it was we came to the point where we just stopped."

The fact that these con artists take advantage of their unsuspecting victims this way, accomplishes three things for the Scammers.

First, because the faultless online group members are offering endorsements based upon what they see as the truth, their support is seen as more trustworthy.

Second, it helps provide what marketers call Social Proof[45] for the legitimacy of the Scammers' programs. Social proof encourages people to look at themselves as being similar to the people around them and doing the same things as the people around them. In social media, for example, "A user on Twitter with a million followers is perceived as more trustworthy and reputable than a similar user with a thousand followers, resulting in faster growth of followers and higher engagement and click-through-rates."[46]

Third, the *deliberate* use of this technique shows just how bad these "dirt-wagons" really are.

Now, there's another important point to remember when it comes to testimonials from people who tell you how very successful they are—along with how they got that way.

Nobody who has a successful home-based business wants other home-business hopefuls to know who they are, or what they sell!

Think about it.

If you were running a very successful million-dollar business from home, would you walk into a room full of people who want to do the same thing and *tell* them *what* you were doing, *how* you were doing it and *what* you were selling?

Of course not! That would be creating *a whole room full of instant competition*! Given the choice, most people will simply copy a successful business rather than go to the trouble of creating their *own* success.

That actually happened to *me*, many, many years ago, when I first started teaching people how to run an online business from home.

Back then, I used one of my own successful websites as a model for the proper way to build and run a product sales website.

When I first started giving away that free information, I had very little competition in that market. My site was doing very well. A year later, there were more than *60* websites *that were exact copies of my site*, right down to the images, my product descriptions and marketing text, and my SEO (search engine optimization factors).

I had to shut the site down, because at that point the search engines had no idea what to do with all those copies, and nobody could make any sales.

So, whenever you see these Scammers using examples of "real people" who tell you what they do and how well they do it, keep in mind that those aren't "real success stories" at all.

In *one way or another*, they are Shills, shoved in your face for the sole reason of getting you emotionally excited about picking up the biggest rock you can lift and dropping it on your foot.

Here's another example that Mike and Sandy shared with me. It's taken from a video produced by the very people who reportedly scammed them—*people who are still out there*, trolling for those who've been told they can easily get rich selling products on sites like eBay and Amazon.com.

In the video, Mike claims the marketer says, ""I'm being joined by my beautiful girlfriend for yet another interview where she's gonna share with you guys a little bit more about her experience. She's gonna share with you guys her first product or second product or third product that she has now launched and selling on Amazon and I'm gonna share with you guys some of my products."

What?? This yahoo wants us to believe that he's going to *destroy* his girlfriend's business *and* his own business by telling hundreds of thousands of people what they both sell, and creating a flood of instant competition?

Uh…no. These people aren't idiots. They're just liars.

Shills are there to hurt you.

Recognize them for what they are.

7 THE COME ON

Social researchers say that all con games are "built on two key elements: the acquisition of the 'Mark's' trust...and the bait—an attractive reward that lures and disarms the 'Mark'."[47]

When a member of a "con-mob" tosses out bait—pitching the beginning of the Long Con to the Mark—that action is often called "The Come On."

If you've been exploring home-based businesses, you've seen and heard lots of Come Ons.

In the case of my student Ivan, Grifters in the con mob wanted to make him think that custom apps--the bait--were the key to making money easily and fast. According to Ivan, ""They were pushing apps," Ivan said, "supposedly these magic apps that'll find the process, the perfect products. A bunch of apps that promised to make me rich quick."

Some of the e-commerce-business-opportunity work-at-home-scheme Grifters also like to use exotic phrases that are designed to make you think they've found a powerful, exclusive, original, new way to make lots of quick cash.

My student Mark described his encounter with the "exotic" phrases" concept this way, "They were really kind of pitching this, you know, saying, oh, we know people who are making $10,000 a month doing nothing but 'retail arbitrage.'"

What? "Retail arbitrage?" I'll explain more about that "exotic" term later.

Mike and Sandy, meanwhile, were dealing with a YouTube Scammer/Grifter/Roper/Shill whose expertise included convincing Marks that they could make tens of thousands of dollars while working for just a short time every day.

According to Sandy, "He's the one who connected us and started on this thing, like, how we could make $50,000 in a month, build a million-dollar business. It goes on and on and on and on...."

And my student Joanell experienced a "Come On" that was full of assurances that never materialized. She says, "There were always promises that you know, they'd give you information and how they were going to help you. But in the end, you were really not getting anywhere with it."

Promises, promises. Always having to do with how much money you'll make, how quickly you'll make it, how much other people have made, and how easy it will be for you.

Come Ons are emotionally charged arrows, carefully sharpened and fired directly at your "Gimme!" button. Yes, you have one, just like every other human being who ever lived.

They're rapid-fired at you with words that push your Gimme!

button over and over again, like claustrophobic ferrets stuck in a broken elevator.

You'll see words like these:

Amazing	Incredible	Rich
Awesome	Independent	Secret
Cash	Ninja	Shocking
Confidential	Profit	Surprising
Earnings	Progress	Unbelievable
Easy	Prosper	Wealthy
Hidden	Prosperous	
	Revenue	

...and a whole lot more.

You can save yourself a big headache by literally writing down these Gimme! Button words and keeping them close to your tablet or keyboard.

It's not just the Come On pitches that use these words. Many of these greed-wracked hacks actually incorporate many of these words into the actual names of their scam products.

Whenever you see words like these in a Come On or in the name of a "business opportunity," run in the other direction.

This is non-negotiable. There's no "but maybe this one is different," or "I dunno, these people seem legit."

Home-based-e-commerce-business-opportunity marketing that plays on your emotions—like your desire for money and success—is marketing with no substance whatsoever.

In other words, if it were real, they wouldn't need to fool you like that. Real opportunities speak for themselves and don't need a sales pitch full of oral flatulence.

Please read the following statements carefully: Any "business opportunity" marketer who has to resort to Gimme! Button words in order to sell something, *has nothing of value to sell.* Any "business opportunity" marketer who talks about dollar amounts has nothing of value to sell.

Not ever.

I've just given you two of the easiest ways to recognize a scam.

Ignore those preceding statements at your own peril.

Here are some examples to help you remember:

When it comes to Gimme! Button words, remember the case of the Bowser brothers, who—according to the FTC—falsely claimed that people who bought their system would learn "secrets for making money on Amazon" and likely earn thousands of dollars a month?[48]

Well, here's an example of how a Gimme! Button word can make its way into the name of a product—in this case—what the Bowsers called their "Amazing Wealth System."

There are likely many other "Amazing" systems being marketed today and you need to look out for them, because as I said, any "business opportunity" marketer who has to resort to "'Gimme! Button" words in order to sell something, has nothing of value to sell.

There's something doubly relevant in the Bowser case. Not only did the Gimme! Button word, "Amazing," show up in the name of their product, the Defendants allegedly used what the FTC called "unsubstantiated earnings claims," which—if proven in any FTC court case—are illegal.

In its court Claim against the Defendants, the FTC said they made basically false statements like "Get started on Amazon and Make $5,000-$10,000 in the next 30 days…even if you have never sold anything online before."

Though they didn't admit to the unsubstantiated earnings charges, the Amazing Wealth System Defendants settled with the FTC and were banned from marketing and selling business opportunities, business-coaching services and making false earnings claims. We'll see.

It may be worth reminding you at this point, that it's not hard for Scammers to use different names and form new corporations with partners—domestic and/or international—who don't have a bust record with the FTC.

That's one reason these work-at-home-e-commerce-business-opportunities pop up again like mushrooms after a rain, especially given the fact that the FTC has enforcement or administrative responsibilities relating to more than 70 laws, with just over a thousand people to do the job and a budget roughly equaling the total of what some of the alleged Scammers in this book earned illegally, before they were stopped.

Another example of a "business opportunity" marketer—allegedly making claims about how people could earn specific dollar amounts—comes from the Federal Trade Commission's court complaint against Digital Altitude and other companies.

In the agency's Complaint, there was an ad that touted huge earnings in a short amount of time. Let's take a look:

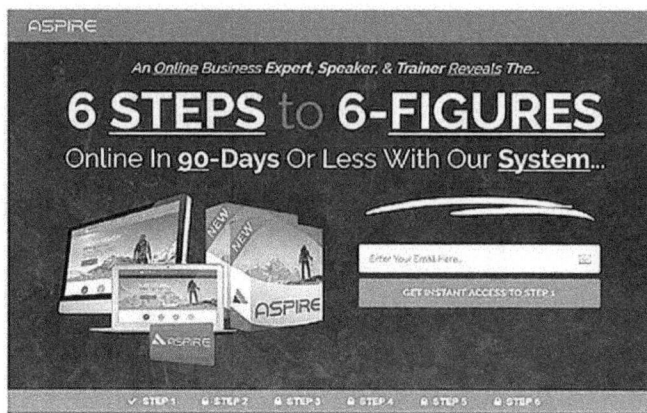

Here's what the FTC had to say about the use of that preceding advertisement for the Defendants' so-called "Aspire System" and related products:

> 32. The main focus of Defendants' advertisements—whether placed on a website, social media platform, or elsewhere, and whether placed by Defendants directly or by consumers using Defendants' marketing materials—is a representation that consumers will quickly make substantial earnings with Defendants' program. For example, the advertisements frequently claim that, with Defendants' program, consumers will "make six figures online in the next ninety days or less."

So what's wrong with that? Plenty. The FTC (the legal Federal Trade Commission) claimed that statements and ads like the preceding one were violations of the FTC Act, because the earnings representations were—again--false, misleading, or were not substantiated.

Rounding out just three examples of "business opportunity"

marketers who got in trouble talking about the dollar amounts their customers might be expected to earn (using worthless systems) are the cases—again—of Sellers Playbook/Exposure Marketing Company and their owners.

The marketing practices of those defendants allegedly violated a total of two Minnesota laws and no less than three Federal laws.

In the case of Sellers Playbook and company, the dollar amounts of allegedly claimed potential earnings were huge.

According to the court claim jointly filed by the FTC and the State of Minnesota, shortly after forming Sellers' Playbook, the Defendants "began deceptively marketing, distributing, promoting, and selling the "Sellers Playbook" business opportunity. Here's an excerpt from the court claim that describes the dollar amounts involved, during what appears to be a live marketing Come On:

Beginning Of Excerpt:[49] *(Court documents following)*

23. Typical earnings claims made in Defendants' advertising and marketing include the following:

    A.   "There are 100,000 Amazon Sellers with sales of $100,000 or more in 2016."

    B.   "[W]e're going to talk about some strategies this afternoon that's [sic] going to show you how to make 15 to 30 percent. Tomorrow, I'm going to go through more wholesaling, and I'm going to teach you guys how to start making anywhere from 20 to 35, 40 percent. On Sunday, we're going to talk about private labeling. Private label, we start making anywhere from 40 to 60 percent. And I've seen a lot of our people making over 70 percent. Now, is 70 percent a good rate of return?"

    C.   "Holy cow, guys. That's when you start seeing the returns of what we want you to have, $20,000 a month."

    D.   "Potential Net Profit: $1,287,463.38."

    E.   "Starting with $1000…1 year later over $210,000."

24. Defendants' earnings claims regarding the business opportunities are false or unsubstantiated.

25. Few, if any, consumers who purchase Defendants' business opportunities earn the income Defendants advertise.

End of Court Claim Excerpt

You now know to avoid marketers who use Gimme! Words, but there's something else you should know about avoiding those marketers who reference specific dollar amounts.

They're sometimes charged with breaking the law if they cannot substantiate an earnings claim, but what you may not know is that if it's a scheme that depends upon you recruiting others in order to get paid—and you do somehow manage to recruit others using the Scammers' marketing materials—you too could be saying "hello" to legal liability.

And that's not all. In addition to violating the FTC Act by misrepresenting earnings potential, or deliberately leaving out important facts, there are at least three other acts in the "big four" line-up of Federal laws that scam marketers violate all of the time. You need to learn about them to protect yourself and also know what to do if you have been scammed. That's something I'll address later in the book.

The second regulation is called the Business Opportunity Rule, which has been around since 2012. Among other protections, it too, is supposed to prevent sellers from making false earnings claims, particularly with regard to work-at-home businesses.

So, what's a business opportunity? In its Claim against Sellers' Playbook, the FTC described a "business opportunity" this way:

"Under the (Business Opportunity) Rule, a 'business opportunity' means a 'commercial arrangement' in which a 'seller solicits a prospective purchaser to enter into a new business;' the 'prospective purchaser makes a required payment;' and the 'seller…represents that the seller or one or more designated persons will…provide outlets, accounts, or customers, including, but not limited to, Internet outlets, accounts, or customers, for the purchaser's goods or services.'"

Internet outlets those sellers offer like Amazon.com? Hmmm…

Regardless, if a company is selling you a "business opportunity," it's not only required to avoid false or unsubstantiated earnings claims, but it's also required to give you—at least seven days before you pay anything—a one-page disclosure document that includes—in short—information that identifies the seller, tells you about lawsuits it's involved in, explains the terms under which the deal can be cancelled or refunded, documents any earnings claims and gives you references.

It's doubtful that many scam marketers will be dumb enough to actually refer to their systems as "business opportunities," but that doesn't mean the FTC and state regulators won't put them under the microscope if they're caught.

The third regulation—in the "big four" Federal regulations designed to protect consumers—is relatively new and it will be a welcome relief for anyone who's asked to sign an agreement promising that he/she won't criticize the Scammer's system in exchange for an allowed refund.

This rule is called The Consumer Review Fairness Act of 2016. In brief, it protects your right to publicly complain about a Scammer, as long as you don't share any of the alleged con artist's confidential information if you do.

Finally, there's the Telemarketing Sales Rule. I'll talk about that later, when I address the nightmarish subject of "boiler rooms."

For now, it's time to look at some of the many ways Come Ons manifest themselves.

EMAILS

As I said earlier, your email address is on email lists. Once it gets on one scam marketer's list, it will be sold and traded, like bottles of water in a drought, to other scam marketers. To Scammers, active email addresses are like gold nuggets.

Money and marketing favors will change hands behind the scenes, commissions will fly back and forth and droves of Scammers, "Ropers" and other members of con-mobs will flood your inbox with a crap-slide of home-based-business horrors.

My student Sharon discovered that it wasn't just other members of the "email address exchange club" who were likely to spam, but even those from whom she'd once requested information.

Sharon says, "Yeah, I was on his email list for something that I got from him. It seemed like every week he was sending, in his email newsletter, a new thing, a different opportunity."

If you haven't figured it out already, starting a real business that earns a full-time income takes time, learning, patience and hard work. There are no shortcuts, although the Scammers would like you to think that there are.

Here's a very basic example of one of these "here's the shortcut" emails. This is based on an actual email supplied by someone, who lost over $30,000 to one of these evil clowns. I've highlighted the emotionally charged Gimme! words and phrases in this email:

100 Profitable Products To Sell on Amazon Get It now!

Hey, I've got something for you today that you're going to LOVE!

So as I'm sure you already know... the first step to building any business is deciding WHAT to sell. How'd you like to SKIP that step and jump straight to making money?

My friends at (Amazing Scamming System) are back and they've just released a FREE training video on how to select the PERFECT product to sell on Amazon.

Even better, they've used all their knowledge and experience of what really works to pick 100 HOT product opportunities. They're giving this list to you for FREE.

THIS is the training that has helped my girlfriend and I get started selling physical products on Amazon and has changed our lives.

I can't recommend them enough... make sure you watch the video and get their bonuses right away.

=> CLICK HERE to get the list and free training video right now.

P.S. Whatever you do, make sure you get all the free bonuses they're giving you with this video. For example, they've also included a list of categories to absolutely avoid if you want to build a $100,000 per month business FAST with Amazon.

GIMME!

"Profitable Products." "Skip that step and jump straight to making money." "Perfect products." "Hot products." "Changed our lives." "Bonuses, bonuses." "$100,000 per month FAST."

Yada-yada blurt-blurt-blurt, ad nauseum.

These are more of the things you need to learn and recognize in the absolute avalanche of poisonous emails that can come sliding your way.

Here's an idea: In self-defense, why not make a game of it? Every time you get an email from one of these snakes, try to pick out the Gimme! words and phrases. If you do that, you'll be far less likely to get bitten and you might even have some fun.

I want to talk for a moment now about that word "Free." Yes, it can be part of a Come On, but the word "Free" is used in lots of marketing and it's OK, as long as what comes after the free stuff is legitimate.

Students Mike and Sandy will never know if an offer made to them for bonus free products was legitimate, because the products never arrived.

According to Sandy, "Basically, we signed up and once we got our receipt, we're supposed to send him a copy. And then he was going to give us all this free stuff. And that didn't happen either."

So while "Free" is a Gimme! word, it's only when a promise of "Free" doesn't materialize or leads you into debt captivity—with nothing to show for it—that it becomes a problem.

Come Ons can also play on other emotions that push your Gimme! Button.

One of the most common Gimme! triggers is the fear of losing a "limited time" opportunity. These are the "scarcity plays" we talked about earlier, and they will always have a short-term deadline.

I want to show you an example of a Come On email containing a scarcity play. Again, I've highlighted the Gimme! words, this time, the words and phrases that can be the tip off to a scarcity play. I've substituted "CrapFest" for the actual name:

50% Off (CrapFest) Ends This Weekend

I want to keep this email brief and to the point, so here's the deal:

In honor of (CrapFest's) one-year anniversary, I'm giving you 6 months of (CrapFest) for the price of 3 — that's 50% off.

The LOWEST price I've EVER offered for (CrapFest) Seriously, we didn't give away a deal this good even during our original launch.

AND I'm doubling my price-back guarantee to 60 days... So you have DOUBLE the time to decide and get your money back in full.

That means you have over 180 days to play with (CrapFest) and 60 days to play with it and get every cent back if you don't like it (which you will because it's the most powerful business software on the planet).

This means you have so much more time to explore what (CrapFest) can do for you and with the doubled price-back guarantee, it's totally RISK-FREE.

BUT — This offer ends THIS WEEKEND, when the timer hits zero.

There's not a ton of time left. Get CrapFest for half the price now.

So, the Scammer promises you'll have lots of time to do all kinds of things…but you'd better start right now, or you lose it. That's a scarcity play.

There are obviously other Gimme! words and phrases in that email, but I focused on the scarcity play this time.

Make no mistake about it; scarcity plays are a marketing gimmick and are used by legitimate companies—as well as con artists—to market their products and services.

Again, in the legitimate world, it could be as simple as a BOGO sale at the supermarket or a limited-time coupon for $2 off laundry detergent.

Scarcity plays are so common that when the Scammers use them, they just blend into all of the marketing that people are used to seeing all the time, and they don't look unusual or out of place.

However, when legitimate companies use the scarcity play, it's real. There is a limited time offer, and it's over with. There will be another limited time offer down the road, but each scarcity play, when used conscientiously, is a real, one-time thing that ends when it says it will and doesn't happen all that often.

The Scammers, though, use the concept of scarcity like your lungs use air. Over and over again, back to back, continuously. It's just one, long, continuous "one time" opportunity that's always "ending", but never does.

What happened once to Mike and Sandy is a good example. Sandy said, "We kept getting this email saying (system name) is going to be closing their doors, you know, and this opportunity is not going to come back around for another year… they really sucker a lot of people in."

Emails containing everything from Gimme! words, to scarcity plays, to "Amazing Success Videos" and much more, occupy a huge role in the Come On. When you get them, study them carefully for Gimme! words and emotional plays of any kind. Whenever you see emails containing Gimme! words and phrases that play on your emotions, *delete them immediately*. You'll save years of wasted time and tens of thousands of dollars.

Come On emails always lead to something I touched on earlier called a Squeeze Page. I'd like you to learn more about Squeeze Pages, so you'll recognize one when you see it.

Squeeze Pages

Squeeze pages are named that, because they're used to "squeeze" you into a "marketing funnel."

Emails, affiliate links, videos and other forms of general online marketing lead to Squeeze Pages. Sometimes a Squeeze Page is found online through its own search engine ranking.

This is another concept that's used by both legitimate and dishonest companies alike and is so familiar to people that they often don't recognize the warning signs that point out the differences between the legitimate use of marketing and a scam.

Here's a very basic, *legitimate* marketing funnel:

Legit Marketing Funnel

Awareness

Interest

Desire

Action

In short, marketing generates Awareness. Awareness leads to Squeeze Pages that create Interest. Interest results in desire. Desire leads to the action, which is the sale.

Now, here's a very basic scam-marketing funnel:

Scam Marketing Funnel

Ropers

Come-On

Long Con

Failure

In the "Scam World" marketing funnel, Ropers, Shills and other con-mob members lead to the Come On.

Then,

1. The Come On leads to
2. The Long Con, which leads to
3. Huge expenditures for useless information that leads to
4. Failure. Always.

It's *the same process*, but instead of legitimate marketing information related to a good product, the scam funnel contains lies, misdirection, Gimme! words, etc., all cons that lead to failure.

Remember the FTC case against the founders of "My Online Business Education (MOBE)?" That was the scheme that—

according to the FTC Complaint—raked in $300 million dollars by allegedly preying on U.S. armed service members, veterans, the elderly and the disabled.

Well, here's an excerpt from that FTC court claim that details the way the alleged Scammers actually used the concept of a funnel system to lure in their Marks:

> 68.   Defendants created and promoted the "Patriot Funnel System," which is also nothing more than a re-branded version of the MOBE program that targets service members and veterans. Defendants launched the website patriotfunnelsystem.com and created ad copies, such as the following, that claim the Patriot Funnel System will reveal "the shocking $97,337 secret a war vet uncovered from his sweat-box room in Afghanistan":

The Scam Squeeze Page can be short or long. Some are a single page in your browser window, and some are long, rambling web pages (you know you've seen them!) that contain all the promises, Gimme! words and other post-digestive horse feed fragments that get you all excited about raiding your kids' college funds to make payments on a scammer's BMW.

Here's a "slightly edited" example of a short, scam squeeze page:

→ **ATTENTION:** BigThinkers, Entrepreneurs, Executives, & Business Owners....Let Us Show You How We Are Generating $22,000 to $147,000 Per Month Online...(part-time) With Our Proven System.

(No B.S. Just Solid Action Plans!)
We are having $10,000 Days and $35,000 Weeks With This...

SEE PROOF & Get Info Now!

Name:

Email:

☑ I have read the Privacy Policy

Free Instant Access

Joe and Mary Buhlschitz

We call it "The Amazing Money Scam!"

PS. If you are broke and/or scared of making ALOT of money this is NOT for YOU! This does cost time, energy and money like any legitimate business.

Except for the substitute "portraits" and Shill names, the preceding is based on a real Squeeze Page.

Do you really need to see any others—short or long?

I didn't think so.

Given the things we've talked about, at this point you should be able to easily spot a Scam Squeeze Page when you see one. And when you start to get all giddy from an overdose of Gimme! words and money promises, STOP, take a few breaths and really think about what you're looking at. Again, doing that will save you lots of time and money.

VIDEOS

I briefly mentioned the Come On video earlier, when we talked about recognizing Ropers. Mansions, fancy cars, money claims, Gimme! words; in scam-video-land, it's all the same thing.

After being bombarded with Come On videos, my student Ivan says he became a near expert at spotting them.

It was an experience my student Ivan doesn't want to repeat, and added, "I honestly, skip every video I hear from now on," Ivan says, "because it's always about a mansion and how it's so easy to do marketing and sales. It was crazy. Like, it got to the point where I had to stop using YouTube because I was getting spammed by all these people."

The Come On video is just a visual version of the emails and Squeeze Pages used by Ropers to pull you into the scam. The videos will often be built right into the emails and squeeze pages.

However, Come On videos are not always so obvious. Ropers will often disguise them as "how to" videos about online marketing, etc.

In legitimate forms of marketing, there are useful "how to" videos about everything from sharpening your lawnmower blades to travel in Asia.

That number also includes a very small number of legit online marketing "how-to" videos. Unfortunately, you never find those few legit marketing videos in search engine results because they're crushed under the tidal wave of scam.

So, you need to recognize scam Come On videos by learning the dead giveaways. As I said, look for mansions, fancy cars, money claims, Gimme! words…you know the drill by now. Watch out for anything extreme that plays on your emotions to get you interested and excited. That's a dead giveaway.

Now, some Ropers and Scammers are getting smarter about their "Come Ons," especially in their Come On videos.

They'll actually start out by appearing very serious and telling you that starting a business is a lot of work and you should never think it's going to be fast or easy.

They'll try very hard to lull you into a false sense of security. ("You're getting veerrryyyy sleepy!")

Don't let your guard down! As soon as you start to think it's safe to dip your toe in the water…BAM! Here come the emotional psyche ploys! Like stray dogs unloading on fire hydrants, they just can't help themselves.

So always watch a video very carefully and look for those emotion-hyping ploys. If you start to see them, run away. Find a video about the nocturnal habits of the Tokay Gecko or something. It may be difficult to turn off the appealing fantasy, but it will cause you a lot less pain in the end.

TELEMARKETERS

Your phone number is the scam marketers' Holy Grail. If they can cold call you (calling out of the blue with no notice), they figure—and perhaps rightly so—that they can talk you into a scam.

If you think that cold calling is an outdated and useless form of marketing, think again. It hasn't gone away; it's just evolved, as the FTC case against the marketers of "8 Figure Dream Lifestyle/ Online

Entrepreneur Academy" demonstrates.

According to an FTC press release,

> "The defendants (who operated in California, Colorado, New York and Tennessee) have used a combination of illegal telemarketing robocalls, live telephone calls, text messaging, internet ads, emails, social media, and live events to market and sell consumers fraudulent money-making opportunities."

The FTC press release confirms that the defendants' strategy worked, as evidenced by consumer losses.

The agency stated that the defendants were often claiming, "…that a typical consumer with no prior skills can make $5,000 to $10,000 in 10 to 14 days and $10,000 or more within 60 to 90 days of buying the program. In reality, the complaint states, consumers who bought the 8 Figure Dream Lifestyle program for between $2,395 and $22,495 rarely earned substantial income, typically lost their entire investment, and often incurred significant loans and credit card debt."[50]

Again, though, there are legitimate telemarketing calls and there are scams. You have to know how to tell the difference. I'm going to repeat it again; dollar-amount earnings claims, emotional plays on your wants and desires, Gimme! words, etc. are the tools the *Scammers always use*.

When you pick up the phone, they'll use an emotional psyche ploy to get you to stay on the phone. Then, the parade starts marching down "Brain Street." They will ask you questions about your personal life and the *specific* things you desire. They do that so they can figure out how to get you emotionally psyched up.

They'll ask you about your financial situation; how much you have in savings, credit, IRA's, etc. They'll call that process a "Business Preparedness Evaluation," or some other ridiculous thing that doesn't exist. This is so they can decide whether they even want to stay on the phone with you. If you tell them you're on a fixed income and can barely make rent, they won't want to waste their precious time. They'll just hang up.

On the other hand, if you tell them that you have good credit, a lot of savings and a high income, they'll never let you go. They'll start to pitch like a Major League ball player.

These telemarketers are Ropers executing a Come On. They're very good. They listen carefully to the tone of your voice and the words you use. They'll adjust the Come On accordingly, as they talk to you.

These people will often sell the same exact thing to one person for $3,500 and to another person for $35,000. They'll have a pre-determined "floor and ceiling" regarding what they can charge. You'll realize that if you keep saying "no," they'll keep dropping the price! They just want to sell you that first thing, some way, any way they can. Because once you're "in the Scam," they can hit you up over and over again.

The telemarketers you talk to are not the people you think they are. They'll tell you they're calling from "The Amazing Incredibly Secret Super-Easy Instant Success University," for example, but they're *not*. They are *contractors* working on a sales-floor-for-hire.

The same telemarketer will be selling e-commerce junk in the morning and real estate junk in the afternoon. They'll work as many telemarketing contracts as they can. They know *nothing* about the actual business they're pitching. They have a general script, and they improvise from there.

They will lie to you. They will comfort you. They will bully you. They'll do whatever they have to do to make that sale, because that sales floor *keeps* a whopping 50 to 80% of every dollar you spend! So, these professional bullshirt artists make huge commissions and are willing to say *anything* to get your money.

When I tell you that Scamming you is big business in this industry, I'm not kidding!

The first person who calls you is known as the "setter." His or her job is to figure out how much money you have and soften you up for the kill shot. Then he or she will ask you to hold while they put the "manager" on the phone. The "manager" is known as the "closer." This specialist is very, very good at executing the actual kill (sale).

If you've let yourself be pulled along through a conversation long enough to actually be transferred to a "closer," it's game over. You don't have a chance.

The pressure in a telemarketing center is intense. That's why they call them "boiler rooms." The telemarketers *must* perform. They are *required* to meet certain monetary goals. Which means, that's all *you* are to them. You're a number. You're money.

So, they'll always insist that you must buy *now* or you're going to lose some imaginary chance at an imaginary "discount price."

These people make a lot of money lying to you, even though—as the complaint filed against the marketing company group Fat Giraffe allegedly illustrates—the FTC's Telemarketing Sales Rule prohibits sellers and telemarketers from "making a false or misleading statement to induce any person to pay for goods or services."[51]

Don't fall for it.

If *you* initiate a call to a company or a person because you have an interest in what they can provide for you, *that's okay*. As long as you pay close attention to the conversation, you can control things. *Do not* buy something on the first call, unless you're *certain* you're comfortable with it and have not been maneuvered into it.

If they initiate a call to you out of the blue, watch out. They're the predator and you're their prey, virtually every time.

INFOMERCIALS

These late-night-TV and cable crap-fests are no different than any other Come On. Take everything I've said in this chapter and put it on TV, and you have the infomercial.

Here's an excerpt from a well-known example of an alleged infomercial scam involving a name many Americans remember; former real estate marketer (who later became the focus of a missing person search) John Beck:

From Reuters (August 28, 2012)[52]

FTC wins $478 million judgment against infomercial scammers

(Reuters) - A U.S. judge has issued a $478 million judgment against the marketers of a series of get-rich-quick real estate infomercials that the Federal Trade Commission said duped almost a million consumers with their claims.

The decision, announced by the FTC on Thursday, marked the largest litigated judgment ever obtained by the agency. It was part of one of several cases the agency has filed as part of its mission to deter scams targeting financial distressed consumers.

"This huge judgment serves notice to anyone thinking of using phony get-rich-quick schemes to defraud consumers," Jeffrey Klurfeld, director of the western region of the FTC, said in a statement.

The FTC filed the lawsuit in June 2009 against the marketers of the three "systems" for making money quick, including "John Beck's Free & Clear Real Estate System." The John Beck system promised to teach consumers how to buy homes for "pennies on the dollar" during government sales, according to the complaint.

But the FTC said the people behind that system and two others made false and unsubstantiated claims about how much money consumers could make using that system and others. Despite the marketing, nearly all buyers of the $39.95 products lost money, the FTC said.

As you can see from the TV graphic that follows, this was a situation involving both infomercials and telemarketing. Need I say more about either? Again—didn't think so!

LIVE MEETINGS

Pre-Covid, there were a large number of "Traveling Circuses" that tramped around from city to city and held "workshops" that were supposed to give you the "Secrets to the Instant Online Work-at-Home Money Tree."

Some of them were small, and others were huge, expensive stage productions. Sometimes they'd cost a few dollars to attend, other times they were free. Whether they were big or small, paid or free, remember this:

These things cost lots of money to stage, but you would not walk away from that meeting with any more real knowledge than you had when you got there, unless you've paid for something expensive while you were there.

Even if you did pay for something, you should know by now that you weren't going to get anything worthwhile out of whatever you paid for.

These things are Come Ons. This is big business for the Scammers. One meeting in a convention hall can *easily* net over a *million dollars* or more for the scams.

I actually attended one of these in Tampa, Florida several years ago at the invitation of one of the vice presidents of the scam company involved in the event.

Why did they invite me? As you already know, I've been in this business for more than 25 years. I have a well-known name. For many, many years, Scammers have approached me and tried to get me to endorse their products and "Rope" my mailing lists for them. I *have never done this and never will*, but I can't do things like write this book if I don't have a lot of first-hand knowledge about how these things work, right?

So, when they invite, I go. Not to help them, but to learn exactly what they're up to so that *I can warn others* through my blog posts, articles, podcasts, eBooks, website and more.

I knew what I was walking into, so I sat way in the back of the room with a notebook (they didn't like people bringing electronic gear into the meeting…they're afraid of being recorded).

They had actually hired a local Tampa TV personality to warm up the crowd. They had him start out by telling some lame jokes. Then he introduced somebody from the company. That person talked about how wonderful life would be if we all bought some $200 app that would help us start a wildly successful home-based online business that would make tons of money overnight.

I wrote the price down in my notebook.

Then that person went away, the TV personality danced around some more, and then introduced another person. *That* person then told us how life would even be *more* wonderful, if we got the *premium* version of whatever they were hawking.

I wrote that price down too.

Once again, dancing TV guy, and *another* company stooge, and *another* wonderful thing we needed to buy right away.

Wrote the price down.

This went on for hours. TV guy, stooge. Wrote the price down. TV guy, stooge. Wrote the price down. There was actually a *lunch break* because the event was so long.

I'll fast forward right to the end of it. When this dog and pony show was over, the numbers in my notebook added up to *over $9,000*. They had carefully fed everybody *just a little bit at a time*, to soften the blow and get everyone so emotionally charged up that they just couldn't wait to line up and pay for everything.

There were "financial advisors" there to take people to computer stations where they would *help them apply for credit cards* so they could pay for all this stuff.

There were "business counselors" there for the people who dared to have doubts about the program and ask questions.

And they raked in the cash by the bucket-load.

At the end, the VP who invited me walked over to me for a discussion. I was struck by the fact that he did not ask me what I thought about the material they were selling. He didn't say a word about the well-being and potential success of his Marks in that meeting.

All he wanted to talk about was how much *money* I could make if I Roped the large numbers of people on my mailing lists into his scam.

I didn't know whether to laugh or to start walking around that convention room and *start warning people not to do it.* (I actually did start walking around and warning people at another one of these things I attended, in Reno, Nevada, but that's another story.)

The *point is* that you know when you walk into one of these things that they're going to try to sell you something. Watch and listen for the emotional psyche ploys, the unrealistic promises and Gimme! words. 99 times out of a hundred, they'll be there. *When you hear them, get up and walk out.* Don't think about it, don't feel like you're missing something and *don't let anybody stop you.* Walk out.

THE BIG GUYS

This may surprise you, but the big, well-known companies you would least suspect, do things that are just as *morally bankrupt* as the people who set out to intentionally scam you.

You see it everywhere you go online. You can barely watch a YouTube video without having to sit through ten seconds of a commercial where some grinning idiot is blabbering "I just built a professional website in 10 minutes with ChikenStix!" (Not the real name, obviously).

This is something I talked about near the very beginning of this book. *Every last online service provider out there thinks you're just too stupid to start and run a real business.* Even the real service providers. They simply see you as a never-ending source of money for their own bottom line.

So they tell you how easy it is. They offer you free trials. They suck you into the system and get you paying them every month for something you don't know how to use. The longer they can string you along, the better for them.

They email you articles about marketing concepts that you don't need and don't know how to do and call it a "newsletter."

Once you're *in* the system, *then* you find out that they have *all kinds of extra* "services, tools and apps" that you need to pay for every month just so you can get the thing to *run* properly, let alone make any money, which you won't.

I've never come across any other pithy saying that describes these big, supposedly reputable companies—as well as the sophisticated smaller Scammers—better than the following:

When I was in high school, I had a very good friend who used to wear a t-shirt that read, "*If you can't dazzle 'em with brilliance, baffle 'em with bullshit.*"

Trying to build a real-income producing business with these people is an automatic fail, because they see you as someone who cannot be taught and they won't even try. They'll just *app* your wallet to death while you wonder what you're doing wrong.

But you're *not* stupid and you're *not* unteachable, so *don't act like it.* Tell them to stick their "free trials, 10-minute websites, services, tools and apps" right back up their own bandwidth and find a different way to learn to run a *real* business *yourself,* like every other *successful* business owner does.

Just because they're big guys doesn't mean you have to let them beat you over the head.

So that's a word or three about the Come On, from companies small and large.

There are also many less obvious ways Scammers will approach you and the best chance you have—to avoid wasting years of your life and tens of thousands of dollars—is very simple: Educate yourself about the predators and their Come Ons.

Remember, aside from staying out of the water—one of the best ways to avoid a shark-attack is to—

Understand how sharks hunt and protect you accordingly.

8 THE SCAM STORE

There's certainly a wide variety of online scams surrounding home-based business opportunities. They masquerade as legitimate offers. They mimic legitimate marketing. Some break laws, others don't. But, in my view, one of the most deplorable things separating scams from legitimate business offerings is this:

The Scammers know that what they offer will not do what they claim.

Some of the offerings in what I call the "Scam Store" will make you some money. The problem is that it won't make you *enough* money to justify the cost you paid for it and the hours you put into it. Even the ones that *can* make *some* money for you simply aren't worth your time.

Imagine working 90 hours a week for an average of $3 an hour, and you'll understand what I mean.

So, let's take a look at some of these grand ideas that people try so hard to shove down your throat—while picking your pocket—and understand why they aren't realistic. From my point of view, that's why they're scams.

The following is partially excerpted from my free *EBiz Insider Video Series, at www.ChrisMalta.com.*[53]

"A successful business owner always researches what *type* of business model is the *most profitable* with the *least investment in time and money and builds a business accordingly.* That's no big revelation; it's simple common sense.

Yet common sense seems to fly out the window when people decide to start a business online.

If you make the *huge* mistake of listening to the Ebiz marketers, they'll have you start an Amazon FBA (Fulfillment by Amazon) business using retail arbitrage while also drop shipping from AliExpress and cross-listing your products on eBay, and then start a website to draw traffic through pay per click advertising to your Amazon and eBay listings that also carry affiliate products and info while building up to private labeling products you import directly from China.

Over time, this utterly counter-productive insanity will cost you tens of thousands of dollars. But they'll tell you it's okay to put tens of thousands on credit cards or refinance your house because you'll make all that money back in just a few months.

Except you won't. You'll *never* make any money that way. The marketers don't care. *They* got paid.

Let's break this down into what works and what doesn't in

the *real* world, and *why*.

From my point of view, that Amazon kind of business can be is a horrible business model for small business. The profit margins can be miserable because you compete against wholesale companies and manufacturers. The rules change on an almost daily basis, so you never know when you're going to get your listings blocked for reasons you don't understand. Amazon routinely blocks entire product lines and brand names for its own reasons, and you can get stuck with a ton of stuff you can't sell.

Although Amazon disputes the idea, I believe that if—as an Amazon merchant—you actually find a product that sells well, Amazon's automatic algorithm may notice that immediately, will take over the niche itself and cut you out of the loop.

The point is that Amazon is *great* for *big* business, but not necessarily small business. Big businesses can live on miniscule profit margins all day because they live on *high volume* and *low margins*. Small business lives on *low volume* and *high margins*, and Amazon's profit margins can be far too small.

Retail arbitrage is not a real thing. Junk marketers made it up a few years ago.

If you think it's a good idea to waste all your time, gas, and energy running around to retail stores all week long, looking for individual bargain products that you then have to package and ship to Amazon to hopefully get resold on FBA for an artificially jacked-up price (which is cheating your own customers), before Amazon figures you out and suspends your account, then retail arbitrage is for you. If you're smarter than that, it isn't.

Arbitrage is a term that refers to *commodities*, not retail products. Gold is a commodity. Grain, precious metals, electricity, oil, beef, and natural gas are all commodities.

An Easy Bake Oven that you have to chase all over town to find on sale and then overcharge for on Amazon is *not* a commodity.

EBiz marketers talk about *"drop shipping"* like it's some kind of unique business system. It isn't. It's nothing more than a product delivery method that's useful when you start out, because you won't have inventory costs.

However, using AliExpress for drop shipping is a huge mistake. You're dealing with drop shippers who *claim* to be in China, but there's no way to be sure of that. You're running a serious risk that those products won't be delivered to your customers at all, and if they are, they can easily be completely different than what was described.

There's no legal recourse for you in China, so if you get screwed, you stay screwed. You're also dealing with delivery times that can range from three weeks to two *months* or more. If your goal is to anger your customers and ruin your reputation, this is a good idea. If not, it isn't. Not *ever*.

Cross-listing your Amazon products on eBay is just plain silly. In fact, using eBay at *all* no longer works. One reason for that; eBay has been encouraging wholesale companies to sell on eBay under assumed seller names since about 2009. That level of price-driven competition leaves no profit margins there either.

Starting a web site to drive traffic to Amazon and/or eBay through paid ads or otherwise, is just as ridiculous as everything else we just discussed. First, that kind of traffic doesn't translate well to Amazon and eBay for reasons we'll discuss later in this video series.

Second, you should never pay for advertising during the startup of your online business. It's an utter waste of money. We have a saying here: "People who start with online advertising are people who don't know how to market online." Natural search engine ranking is much more powerful.

Placing affiliate products on a (physical product sales) web site will hurt that site, as well as your business, by messing up your "search engine optimization."

Affiliate marketing is also a bad idea because you have to do *all* the same work to market an affiliate site as you would to market a site on which you sell the products *yourself.* As an affiliate, you get a small commission. As an actual product site owner, you keep all the profits, for exactly the same amount of work.

Small commission, versus full profits. Not hard to figure out.

Private labeling is yet another Ebiz marketer gimmick. Examine this concept through the eyes of a *businessperson.* If you do, you'll recognize that companies spend tens of millions of dollars to create brands that are recognized by consumers. Why do they do that? Because recognized brands are trusted more and sell much better. What could possibly be the point of spending all the money it takes to grab generic junk from China and slapping an unknown name on it?

That's the *opposite* of branding, and yet again, it's just another gimmick that sounds good but doesn't work.

And then they all talk about importing from China. *Really?* I sent several of my employees to Guangzhou Province in China a while back, to explore this idea. Yes, you can get stuff for very low prices when you're *in* China. It's getting them back to *your* country that's expensive.

If you're going to do that, you have to *go* to China. Then, you have to buy in *huge* quantities to get those low prices, so make sure to bring a truckload of money.

You'll then have to hire an agent in China to look after your interests. After that, it'll take two or three months to have your products made. Then, you pay for shipping by ocean freighter because you have to buy in truckload quantities to get those low prices.

When it reaches your port of entry in the U.S., for example, you have to consult the US Harmonized Tariff Schedule to see how much Import Tax you're going to pay. Then there are Customs fees. Then you have to hire a freight company to transport your stuff to whatever warehouse you're going to pay for to *keep* your stuff in.

Importing from China sounds good when the Ebiz marketers *talk* about it, but they leave a *lot* of stuff *out* of that conversation. Remember that scam marketers often exclude crucial information from their "business opportunities" and victims of their swindles often don't realize that, until they've already spent thousands of dollars on useless information and/or software.

Successful business owners know to *leverage* other people's money. For example, there are already *thousands* of very large wholesale distributors importing *hundreds of billions* of dollars' worth of products from China *into* the US every year. They have far more buying power than you do and get far lower prices than you can!

Let *them* import the products, then buy from them for less than you *ever* could by trying to import by yourself! Again, that's common sense, but the con artists will never tell you that. They make too much money selling you lies about importing from China!

The only thing that *does* make sense is building your own website, but *not* using paid ads, affiliate programs and sending traffic to the flea markets like eBay and Amazon.

Your own website, marketed properly and selling physical products directly to your customers, is and always has been, the most profitable way to make money online. So that's what we'll be talking about here.

I *could* teach you all of that other stuff. I do know how to do it. But I *don't* do it, because it's all a waste of time and money and none of it is good business practice. It makes money for the *marketers*, **not** for you.

(End of video excerpt)

So, there's that Gordian knot again. These Scammers have one scam twisted around another one, twisted around another one, and so on. They will do their absolute best to drag you into as many of them as they can, take all your cash, run you around in circles until you drop, and then laugh about it all the way to the bank.

What I've described here are some of the larger scams. There are also plenty of smaller ones out there.

Regardless of their size, *you don't have to fall for them.*

In the final chapter of this book, I'll summarize the things you need to look for to avoid being sucked into "The Knot" that leaves you hopelessly tied to a mountain of debt.

9 THE TELLS

Dictionary publisher Merriam Webster defines a "tell" (a noun used in the game of poker) as "an inadvertent behavior or mannerism that betrays a poker player's true thoughts, intentions, or emotions."[54]

This isn't poker, but it might as well be! You have to learn to read your opponent's "hand" to know whether you're being scammed or not. In this book, I've already pointed out some of the discussed "Scam Tells," but I thought it might be a good idea to review them to give you easy access to them.

I've also added some information at the end to help you complain about scams and possibly even get your money back if you've been a victim.

This Scam Tells chapter is a short review, really, because most cons are based on the same rudimentary ideas and rooted in simple psychology. Just remember that the *minute* you start looking into starting a home-based business, you are The Mark, and the Scammers are hunting you. No exceptions.

Related to home-based business (selling products or other):

- Anybody who *tells* you that selling on Amazon, as a home-based business owner is an *always*-good idea, is either lying to you or stupid. That also goes for private labeling, retail arbitrage, importing from China and all the other chuckle-bombs these people will try to drop on you. Forget about Amazon. The cost to benefit ratio is too high. It works for big companies, not home-based business owners.

- Anybody who *tells* you that selling on eBay, as a home-based business owner is a good idea is either lying to you or stupid. EBay stopped being a good idea in 2009 (three years after my co-authored book, *What to Sell on eBay and Where to Get It,* was published). Selling on eBay stopped working for home-based businesses when eBay started inviting big wholesalers and manufacturers into the platform, giving them an easier set of rules to live by. The price competition on eBay is now far too extreme.

- Anybody who *tells* you that drop shipping from China as a home-based business owner is a good idea, is—again— either lying to you or stupid, because doing so means you'll be involved with unverified wholesalers, with no legal reciprocity, no returns, weeks-long wait times for delivery, misrepresented products., etc. It's an absolute no-brainer.

- Anyone who *tells* you that you will earn large, specific, amounts of money in short time frames if you get you involved with them is lying to you and may be breaking the law.

- Anyone who *tells* you things using "Gimme!" words in his or her marketing is being deceptive and trying to distract you from looking for signs that the offer is a scam.

- Likewise, anyone who *tells* you things using marketing that strongly plays on your desires and emotions, is being deceptive and trying to throw you off what you should really be looking for.

- Anyone who *tells* you that starting your own business from home is easy is lying to you.

- Anyone who *tells* you that you'll make money quickly is lying to you.

As you spot the Tells, take action:

- Don't fall for Scam Squeeze Pages, scam emails and scam videos. You know how to identify them now; avoid them.

- You know what scam Come Ons are now. Avoid them.

- You know what Scam Infomercials are now. Please watch something else.

- You now know what "live scam workshops and meetings" look like. Do something else.

Remember that you need to *control* what happens to you when encounter the evil clowns, even though it isn't as easy as some might think.

Most of us know when we're being taken for a ride, but carefully orchestrated emotional and psychological pitches can easily create a "Suspension of Disbelief" that can be unbalancing.

Many people who've been exploited don't understand how these cunning, "no-holds-barred," con artists work. That's why they were scammed. It's the same reason that many of the most injured victims—thousands and thousands of dollars later—still don't realize they were victims.

So, ask questions. Look for reviews, but try to search only on legitimate, independent review sites like *Consumer Reports*,[55] the Better Business Bureau (BBB),[56] TrustPilot[57], etc.

Assuming that the publication or website evaluates businesses like the one you're investigating and makes an effort to prevent or weed out fake reviews, the more positive reviews you see for that business or person on those sites, the better.

Look for discrepancies but also be very aware that there are other websites out there, which pose as legitimate review sites, but are actually scams run by swindlers who sometimes actually *feature* bad reviews (think "fake news") in order to try to extort money for modifying or removing even one bad review.

To sum it up, make an effort to know to whom you're talking. Check reputations. Check business name registrations online.

One final point for those who've been "bitten" by these sharks: Refunds will likely be difficult to come by, but that doesn't mean you shouldn't ask.

If you're actually *offered* a refund, make sure you don't have to sign away your right to publicly complain in order to get it. As I mentioned before, your right to complain is now protected by law.[58]

Whether or not you've been offered a refund, if you've been scammed you need to complain. There are many reasons why.

First, by complaining, you can do your part to help bust up the unfair "blame the victim" stereotype in the online-business-opportunity-scam-industry.

Many people believe the myth that people who are scammed "brought it on themselves," but the people who believe that myth don't understand that con artists are experts at taking advantage of human vulnerabilities, like wanting our lives to become better and being willing to explore the new opportunities available because of advancements in technology. In short, if we want our lives to improve, we are *all* potential victims of some type of con.

Second, the more that people complain about the "home-based-e-commerce-or-other-type-of-online-business-scams" the better the chance that more of the Scammers will find it harder to pull in victims. Who knows, more of them might actually be put out of business.

At the end of this book, there's a list of many consumer protection agencies who participate in the Federal Trade Commission's Consumer Sentinel Network (CSN). The actual data reported is only available to law enforcement agencies, but if one of these agencies seems interested in receiving complaints—like the FTC, the BBB, your state attorney general's office or even the U.S. Dept of Justice,[59] or the U.S. Post Office Inspection, [60] (think "mail fraud')—you may want to gather up your paperwork and file a complaint. Even if you don't receive a response right away, you may be doing more good than you know, because your complaint may help with future investigations into the same scammer. People I know have seen this happen first-hand.

As I said earlier, you're probably smarter than any of the people who try to cheat you; and certainly smart enough to take some parting advice from successful business founder T. Boone Pickens, who was known for his "Texas size" personality, controversy and business smarts.

Before his death in 2019, Pickens reportedly said he hoped that he would be remembered for "An undying love for America, and the hope it presents for all...a passion for entrepreneurship, and the promise it sustains."[61]

I might not agree with everything Pickens said and did in his career, but I admire anyone with a love for his country and the courageous business founders who are part of its economic backbone. I also agree with his specific advice to, "Learn to analyze well. Assess the risks and the prospective rewards, and keep it simple."

Now that you know some of what to watch out for, act like it and you'll be fine.

I appreciate that you've taken the time to read this book and I hope you gained some useful information from it.

You can find much more "down-in-the-trenches real-life truth" from my 25+ years in this business at my website, www.ChrisMalta.com,[62] and my **Free EBiz Insider Video Series,** which teaches how selling online really works. Those videos introduce a comprehensive the E-commerce Education I teach; which I firmly believe to be the only real Education that exists in this business.[63]

Safe journey to you. :o)

Supporting Documents

Percentage of Population Involved in Business Start-Ups

Percentage of population involved in business start-ups in the Americas in 2018, by country

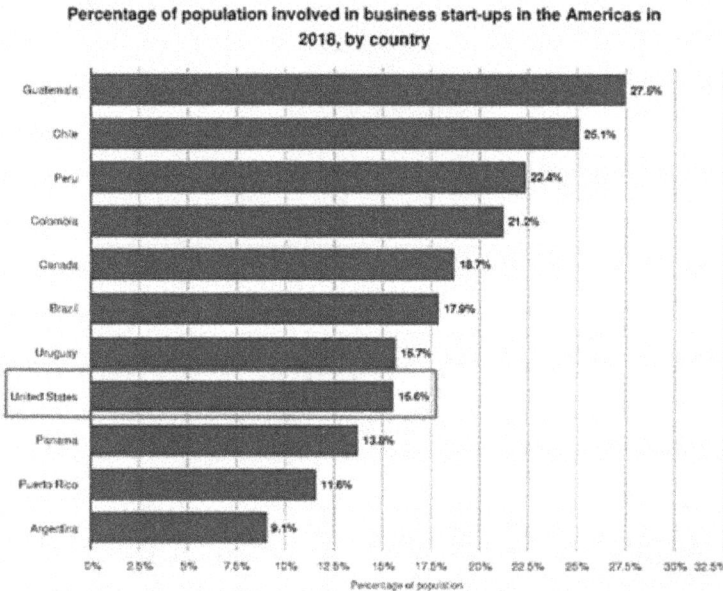

Country	Percentage
Guatemala	27.9%
Chile	25.1%
Peru	22.4%
Colombia	21.2%
Canada	18.7%
Brazil	17.9%
Uruguay	16.7%
United States	15.6%
Panama	13.8%
Puerto Rico	11.6%
Argentina	9.1%

Source
GEM
© Statista 2019

statista

Additional information: North America, Central and South America 2018 data composed of the Adult Population Survey and the National Expert Survey of Adults, Ages 18-64 years (Estimated at 200 million in U.S.). Source: Global Entrepreneurship Monitor (GEM).

These statistics show the total early-stage entrepreneurial activity (TEA) rate in the Americas in 2018, by country. An economy's total early-stage entrepreneurial activity (TEA) rate is defined as the prevalence rate of individuals in the working age population who are actively involved in business startups, either in the phase in advance of the birth of the firm, or the phase spanning 42 months after the birth of the firm. According to data from the Global Entrepreneurship Monitor, in 2018, the early-stage entrepreneurial activity (TEA) rate in the United States was 15.6% percent of the working age population (18-64)

(See U.S. Population Breakdown for 2018 on next page)

U.S. Population Breakdown for 2018			
Total population Over 18 years[64]	Total population over 65 years[65]	Total population ages 18-64[66]	Total population ages 18-64 estimated to be involved in startup businesses[67] (15.6%)
253,768,092	52,000,000	201,768,092	31,475,822

Consumer Sentinel Network
Data Contributors (Partial List)

AARP Fraud Watch Network,
Alaska Attorney General,
Canada Competition Bureau,
Colorado Attorney General,
Consumer Financial Protection Bureau,
Green Dot Corporation,
Hawaii Office of Consumer Protection,
Homeowners Preservation Foundation,
Idaho Attorney General,
Indiana Attorney General
International Association of Better Business Bureaus,
Iowa Attorney General,
Los Angeles County Department of Consumer and
Business Affairs,
Louisiana Attorney General,
Maine Attorney General,
Massachusetts Attorney General,
Michigan Attorney General,

Consumer Sentinel Network
Data Contributors (Partial List, Continued)

Microsoft Corporation Cyber Crime Center,
Mississippi Attorney General,
MoneyGram International,
Montana Department of Justice,
National Consumers League,
Nebraska Attorney General,
Nevada Attorney General,
Nevada Department of Business and Industry,
New York State Attorney General,
North Carolina Department of Justice,
Ohio Attorney General,
Oregon Department of Justice,
Pennsylvania Attorney General,
PrivacyStar,
Publishers Clearing House,
South Carolina Department of Consumer Affairs,
Tennessee Division of Consumer Affairs,
U.S. Department of Defense,
U.S. Department of Education,
U.S. Department of Veterans Affairs,
U.S. Postal Inspection Service,
Utilities United Against Scams,
Washington State Attorney General,
Western Union Company,
Wisconsin Department of Agriculture,
Trade and Consumer Protection,
Xerox Corporation

In addition, the following entities that refer complaints to the FTC (The Federal Trade Commission):

Ayuda,

Catholic Charities USA,

Connecticut Department of Consumer Affairs,

Iowa, Clinton County Sheriff's Office,

Ohio, Cuyahoga County Department of

Consumer Affairs

PeopleClaim

Petscams.com

Scam Detector

U.S. Customs and Border Protection

U.S. Department of Health and Human Services,

Office of Inspector General

U.S. Department of Justice, Disaster Fraud

Task Force

U.S. Department of Justice, Executive

Office for Immigration Review

U.S. Department of Justice,

Task Force on Market Integrity and Consumer Fraud

U.S. Department of the Treasury,

Internal Revenue Service

U.S. Senate Special Committee on Aging

ABOUT THE AUTHOR

Chris Malta is an entrepreneur and pioneer in the field of e-commerce, having spent over 25 years building successful online businesses and teaching others to do the same. His education classes are available at **www.ChrisMalta.com**

Growing up in an entrepreneurial family and getting his start as a young teenager, Chris actually has more than 45 years of overall experience as a successful entrepreneur in the retail, wholesale, service and online industries.

In 1999, Chris became the Founder and CEO of Worldwide Brands, Inc., a Better Business Bureau (BBB) A+ rated wholesale supplier directory for home-based business. He's also presented more than 800 live e-commerce business Workshops online and recently released a comprehensive one-on-one e-commerce Education course that includes and adds to the accepted best practices he's been teaching for several years.

During his 25+ years as an entrepreneur and e-commerce educator, he's offered students more than 7,000 hours of personal business mentoring. He's been a featured speaker at national internet conventions and written several e-commerce books, including one he wrote at eBay's request, which was published by McGraw-Hill.

Chris has worked face-to-face with Amazon and eBay executives, built successful product sales sites and—before some scammers became the star players in the affiliate (referral) marketing world, Chris created an ethical 27,000-member affiliate-marketing program.

He's owned a wholesale distribution company, spent years hosting live business talk radio shows for *Entrepreneur Magazine* and was

Product Sourcing Editor for *eBay Radio*. He's also created hundreds of e-commerce articles as well as videos and podcasts.

Chris says he can't stand working for other people, but was born with what he calls, "that 'wild hair' that just keeps tickling my brain and telling me I have to be my own person, in charge of my own destiny."

Chris recognizes that independent streak in others and says his passion is to help them learn to set up successful e-commerce businesses. Toward that end, he offers his internationally acclaimed, educational 11-part EBiz Insider Video Series, (rated 4.9 / 5 by Trustpilot), free of charge at www.ChrisMalta.com. Yes, really!

In addition to the earlier mention of teaching students the best methods for starting and running an online e-commerce business, Chris spends much of his time educating the public about the good and the dangers of work-from-home e-commerce scams.

END NOTES
INTRODUCTION

[1] https://chrismalta.com/FreeVideoSeries/

[2] https://www.trustpilot.com/review/chrismalta.com

[3] See SUPPORTING DOCUMENTS Graphic: Percentage of Population Involved in Business Start-Ups

CHAPTER 1 - THE HUNT

[4] From *The Confidence Game* by Harvard psychologist Maria Konnikova

[5] FBI annual Internet Crime Report (IC3), 2018

[6] See SUPPORTING DOCUMENTS Graphic, Percentage of Population Involved in Business Start-Ups

[7] May 6, 2019 Atomik Research survey for The UPS Store franchises.

[8] Ibid.

[9] See complete list of Consumer Sentinel Network Data Contributors in SUPPORTING DOCUMENTS

[10] October 1, 2019 FTC Press Release, "Millennials More likely to Report Losing Money to Fraud than Older Generations…

[11] "Half of Americans Prefer Opening a Small Business to Retirement," Atomik Research survey for The UPS Store franchise;

[12] Reports by Military Consumers; Consumer Sentinel Data Book, 2018

[13] Orbach, Barak, and Lindsey Huang. "Cons and Scams Their Place in American Culture." *Social Research International Quarterly*, vol. 85, no. 4, pp. 795–796. Winter 2018. Classic types of confidence games: Gold-Brick Scams, Multilevel Marketing Schemes.

[14] U.S. Senate Appropriations Subcommittee Hearing on Proposed FTC Budget Estimates for FY2020, May 7, 2019

[15] According to the FTC complaint, Defendants conducted Sellers Playbook live events throughout the United States including in Albuquerque, Anaheim, Anchorage, Atlanta, Atlantic City, Austin, Baltimore, Boise, Boston, Buffalo,

Charleston, Charlotte, Chicago, Cincinnati, Cleveland, Columbus, Dallas, Denver, Des Moines, Detroit, El Paso, Fort Lauderdale, Fort Myers, Fort Wayne, Fort Worth, Grand Rapids, Hartford, Honolulu, Houston, Indianapolis, Jacksonville, Kansas City, Las Vegas, Lincoln, Long Beach, Long Island, Los Angeles, Louisville, Memphis, Miami, Milwaukee, Nashville, New York City, Newark, Norfolk, Oklahoma City, Orlando, Palm Springs, Philadelphia, Phoenix, Pittsburgh, Raleigh, Reno, Richmond, Sacramento, Salt Lake City, San Antonio, San Diego, San Francisco, San Jose, Seattle, Saint Louis, Tampa, Tucson, Washington DC, and Wichita.
Source: Page 22 of https://www.ftc.gov/system/files/documents/cases/sellers_playbook_complaint.pdf.

CHAPTER 2 - THE GRIFTERS

[16]https://www.merriam-webster.com/dictionary/grift

[17] https://www.cnet.com/news/ftc-gets-11m-settlement-from-get-rich-quick-scammers-targeting-amazon/

[18] https://www.ftc.gov/news-events/press-releases/2018/06/operators-get-rich-amazon-scheme-settle-ftc

[19]https://www.ftc.gov/system/files/documents/cases/de_080_entered_stipulated_order_for_permanent_injunction_and_monetary_ju._.pdf

[20] https://www.cnet.com/news/ftc-charges-alleged-sham-get-rich-quick-coaches-targeting-amazon/

[21] https://www.cnet.com/news/amazon-continues-crack-down-on-alleged-fake-reviews-site/

[22] https://www.cnet.com/news/amazon-sues-alleged-counterfeit-sellers/

[23] https://www.cnet.com/news/amazon-tries-to-snuff-out-a-bunch-of-kindle-publishing-scams/

[24] https://www.ftc.gov/

CHAPTER 3 - THE MARK

[25] Orbach, Barak, and Lindsey Huang. "Cons and Scams Their Place in American Culture." Social Research International Quarterly, vol. 85, no. 4, p. 797. Winter 2018.

[26] Ibid. P. 797

[27] https://www.ftc.gov/news-events/blogs/business-blog/2019/02/fat-giraffe-marketings-ads-truth-was-endangered-species

[28] Orbach, Barak, and Lindsey Huang. "Cons and Scams Their Place in American Culture." Social Research International Quarterly, vol. 85, no. 4, p. 797. Winter 2018.

[29] https://en.wikipedia.org/wiki/Suspension_of_disbelief

CHAPTER 4 - THE ROPERS

[30] U.S. Senate Appropriations Sub Committee Hearing; Proposed Budget Estimates for FTC FY2020, May 7, 2019

[31] https://www.ic3.gov/crimeschemes.aspx#item-7

[32] https://news.harvard.edu/gazette/story/2019/04/harvard-grad-studies-cons-and-how-to-avoid-them/

[33] Mayo Clinic definition of Narcissistic Personality Disorder.

CHAPTER 5 - THE LONG CON

[34] https://en.m.wikipedia.org/wiki/Madoff_investment_scandal

[35] https://en.m.wikipedia.org/wiki/Ponzi_scheme

[36] Federal Trade Commission, Plaintiff, v. MOBE Ltd., United States District Court Middle District of Florida Civil Action Number: 6:18-cv-862-ORL-37DCI

[37] https://en.wikipedia.org/wiki/Confidence_trick#Short_and_long_cons

[38] Orbach, Barak, and Lindsey Huang. "Cons and Scams Their Place in American Culture." *Social Research International Quarterly*, vol. 85, no. 4, pp. 801. Winter 2018

[39] Federal Trade Commission, Plaintiff, v. MOBE Ltd., United States District Court Middle District of Florida Civil Action Number: 6:18-cv-862-ORL-37DCI

[40] https://ideas.ted.com/dont-get-fooled-or-conned-again-here-are-the-5-tactics-to-look-out-for/

CHAPTER 6 - THE SHILL

[41]https://www.ftc.gov/news-events/press-releases/2014/02/ftc-halts-multi-million-dollar-work-home-business-coaching-scheme

[42]https://www.ftc.gov/system/files/documents/cases/140224applyknowledgecmpt.pdf

[43] https://www.ftc.gov/news-events/press-releases/2018/04/defendants-who-took-part-business-coaching-scheme-settle-ftc

[44] Orbach, Barak, and Lindsey Huang. "Cons and Scams Their Place in American Culture." Social Research International Quarterly, vol. 85, no. 4, p. 802. Winter 2018.

[45] Cialdini, R. B. (1984). Influence: The Psychology of Persuasion

[46] https://en.wikipedia.org/wiki/Social_proof#In_social_media

CHAPTER 7 - THE COME ON

[47] Orbach, Barak, and Lindsey Huang. "Cons and Scams Their Place in American Culture." Social Research International Quarterly, vol. 85, no. 4, pp. 795. Winter 2018. Classic types of confidence games: Gold-Brick Scams, Multilevel Marketing Schemes.

[48] https://www.ftc.gov/news-events/press-releases/2018/03/ftc-action-halts-large-deceptive-business-opportunity-scheme
[49] FTC and STATE OF MINNESOTA v. SELLERS PLAYBOOK, INC., EXPOSURE MARKETING COMPANY CASE 0:18-cv-02207-DWF-TNL

[50] https://www.ftc.gov/news-events/press-releases/2019/06/ftc-law-enforcement-partners-announce-new-crackdown-illegal

[51] UNITED STATES DISTRICT COURT DISTRICT OF UTAH, CENTRAL DIVISION, Case No.19-cv-00063 (CW)

[52] https://www.reuters.com/article/us-ftc-infomercial/ftc-wins-478-million-judgment-against-infomercial-scammers-idUSBRE87M13520120823

CHAPTER 8 – THE SCAM STORE

[53] https://chrismalta.com/FreeVideoSeries/

CHAPTER 9 – THE TELLS

[54]https://www.merriam-webster.com/dictionary/tell

[55] https://www.consumerreports.org/cro/index.htm

[56] https://www.bbb.org/search

[57] https://www.trustpilot.com/

[58] U.S. Consumer Review Fairness Act of 2016

[59] https://www.justice.gov/usao/us-attorneys-listing

[60] https://www.uspis.gov/

[61] https://boonepickens.com/?p=2343

[62] https://chrismalta.com/

[63] https://chrismalta.com/FreeVideoSeries/

Percentage of Population Involved in Business Start-Ups (Chart)

[64] SOURCE: U.S. Census Bureau Estimates of the Total Resident Population and Resident Population Age 18 Years and Older for the United States, States, and Puerto Rico: July 1, 2018

[65] SOURCE: Population Reference Bureau: https://www.prb.org/aging-unitedstates-fact-sheet/

[66] Total population over 18 minus total population over 65

[67] Total population ages 18-64 multiplied by 15.6%

www.ingramcontent.com/pod-product-compliance
Lightning Source LLC
Chambersburg PA
CBHW022111280326
41933CB00007B/345